How To Make Money In The Stock Market With Minimal Risk And High Returns

A Complete Step By Step Guide To A Long Term Investing Approach That Beats The Market

BRIAN DEEKER

(www.briandeeker.com)

HOW TO MAKE MONEY IN THE STOCK MARKET WITH MINIMAL RISK AND HIGH RETURNS

Copyright © 2019 by Brian Deeker.

For information contact :

https://www.briandeeker.com

Book and Cover design by Brian Deeker Publishing

ISBN: 978-0-578-49116-5

First Edition: April 2019

CONTENTS

INTRODUCTION

The purpose of this book is to teach you how to invest wisely in the stock market without losing any money. This is new information which has never been presented before. I have written this book to be as concise as possible so that you don't have to struggle through endless pages of useless information as is the case with most investment books that really don't provide any information on how to invest to beat the market.

If you are looking for information on how to invest quickly, then this book is not for you as my approach is long-term, often over many years. However, the returns are exceptional (with built in tax advantages), and the risk is minimal.

This book is not a get rich quick book. It is designed to give you the foundation that you need to be able to make wise financial investments. I will show you how to take control of your financial future and set yourself up for long term success as a stock market investor.

The finance industry is set up so that investing in the stock market appears complicated. It's not. Fund managers have set it up this way so that they can charge you the outrageous fees that they routinely get away with. There are many financial traps that are intentionally laid for the unwary and the industry is full of well-meaning individuals who simply don't know what they are doing. Even worse, there are genuine sharks out there that want your money and know exactly how to get it from you.

The finance industry is the only industry where you are better off doing it yourself. You wouldn't pull your own teeth or give yourself legal advice, but the finance industry is so corrupt that you are better off choosing your investments by throwing darts at a dart board covered with stock symbols. You will get about the same return with none of the fees.

I buy companies in the Mid Cap, Large Cap and Mega Cap lists of companies that trade on the New York Stock Exchange (NYSE) as the foundation for making my stock selections and then compare my results with the returns of the S&P 500. The S&P 500 is a list of the top 500 companies in the US, prepared each year by Standard & Poor, and has averaged 7.95% average annual return since its inception in 1957. It is the bench mark that all fund managers measure their results against.

In 1993, the SPDR® S&P 500® ETF (SPY Exchange Traded Fund) was introduced by State Street Global Advisors, which mimics the S&P 500 and is a way for investors to invest with the same returns and the same companies as the S&P 500. Until the fund was introduced, there was no way to invest in the S&P 500 other than buying all the stocks at the same percentages as the S&P 500.

According to a study called *Fleeting Alpha: Evidence From the SPIVA and Persistence Scorecards* by Ryan Poirier, FRM and Aye M. Soe, CFA of the S&P Dow Jones Indices, 95% of fund managers cannot beat the S&P 500. The fund managers that do beat the S&P 500 in any given year are rarely the same each year.

Robert Arnott, an industry expert and founder of Research Affiliates spent two decades studying the top 200 actively managed mutual funds that have at least $100 million in assets under management. From 1984 to 1998, only eight of the 200 fund managers beat the Vanguard 500 index, which is an index put together by Jack Bogle that is a mirror image of the S&P 500 index. That is an incredible 96% of fund managers that can't beat the S&P 500.

Many financial experts will tell you that it is impossible to beat the S&P 500, so why even try?

I am here to tell you that you can beat the S&P 500 because I have done it. I have earned an average annual return of 13.54% since the beginning of 2010, while the S&P 500 returned 9.91% during the same period. I developed a system that takes a conservative, long term approach to investing that uses the financial data that every company is required to provide to the Securities and Exchange Commission (SEC). This financial data is public record and is regularly audited by independent sources. This information provides a clear indication of the financial health of the companies that I invest in, showing me when to buy and sell the stocks.

I have back tested my investment approach from 1980 to the

beginning of 2019 using stocks that are in the S&P 500 and achieved an average annual return of 11.75% during that time. I used publicly available historical data for stock prices, dividend and earnings data to make my stock selections. Obviously, I didn't start trading in 1980 as a nine-year-old, but what I did do was apply my principles the same way as I do for my own investment decisions, without prior knowledge of future stock prices.

I also back tested my approach using stocks in the S&P 500 against the SPDR® S&P 500® ETF (SPY) to give you a more realistic comparison since you could buy the SPY from the beginning of 1993.

If you had invested $1 million in the SPY in January 1993, you would have $6.15 million in your account as of March 5th, 2019 and your average annual return would have been 8.44% - not a bad return and certainly better than most fund managers. With my investment approach, using only companies in the S&P 500, $1 million invested at the beginning of 1993 would have yielded a 9.44% average annual return and you would have had $7.65 million in your account as of March 5th, 2019, a significant difference of $1.5 million. Exact figures are outlined in the table below:

	Start Amount	End Amount	Dividend Amount
SPY	$999,973 [1]	$6,151,139	$1,392,552 [2]
My Results	$999,928 [3]	$7,655,411	$2,666,508 [4]

[1] The start amount was worked out using the buy price of the SPY on 3/31/1993 of $45.34 and multiplying it by 22,055 shares to get the start amount slightly under $1 million since you can't buy partial shares.

² The dividend amount was worked out by totaling the recorded dividend amount for each share ($63.14) from 3/31/1993 to 3/5/2019 and multiplying this figure by the 22,055 shares. The dividend is included in the SPY share price and cannot be withdrawn.

³ I started with 40 stocks and divided the starting amount equally among the stocks. The figure of $999,973 accounts for whole stocks only, since you can't buy part of a stock. Commissions payable to the broker would have totaled $278 but have not been included as part of the study since the overall difference is negligible at less than $1,000 in commission fees.

⁴ The dividends were calculated from public records and would have been available as an additional income stream without having to sell any stocks. The dividends could also have been re-invested during market collapse for a much higher overall return. Profits from the dividends were not re-invested during market crashes as part of this study.

In the same time period, Berkshire Hathaway, the investment company owned by Warren Buffett (recognized as the world's greatest investor) and Charlie Munger had an average annual return of 9.56% compared with my return of 9.44% (using only stocks in the S&P 500). Warren Buffett is 88 years old at the time of this writing and Charlie Munger is 94. The company hasn't named their successor yet and many investors are uneasy about the future of Berkshire Hathaway. You could invest in Berkshire Hathaway for $302,200 per share as of March 5th, 2019 and get similar results as I have achieved, or you can follow the advice written in this book.

This method works, you be the judge. Whether you have millions to invest or can barely spare $250 a month, this investment approach will work for you.

No part of this book is intended to provide legal advice and I am not legally responsible for any trading that you choose to do. I am here as your guide and this book is written to teach you how I invest.

CHAPTER ONE

Why It Is So Important to Become an Investor

Many people have entered the stock market with high expectations but have failed miserably and often lose all their initial investment. However, it doesn't have to be that way for you.

Investing can be learned by anyone if you take the time to really master the principles. It takes patience, commitment and a willingness to follow a proven system. However, the rewards are incredible, and you will eventually be able to live your life on your own terms, doing what you want, when you want. It is worth the time to learn these skills.

Imagine the day you retire. Is it going to be a joyous occasion, worthy of celebration, or is it going to be a time of fear and dread? How far into the future is it? Are you ready?

If you learn to invest properly, then your retirement will be comfortable and happy, but if you let it creep up on you, you may be forced to take a job at Walmart or Kroger as a greeter or pushing carts just to be able to eat. I see it all the time, but it doesn't have to be that way for you. You can take charge now and have a comfortable and meaningful retirement.

Have you planned for what is coming? Or, are you just going with the flow of life? How much do you really need in retirement anyway? Most financial experts say that you need 15 times your salary in an investment fund. According to the U.S. Census Bureau (www.census.gov), the median household income for 2017 is $60,336, which is the highest it has been since 2007. If these financial experts are correct, then $905,040 (which is $60,336 multiplied by 15 years) in an investment fund is enough to retire on. But, is it really? How much do you need every year to live on?

How much of a return on your retirement nest egg is enough? If you are getting a 5% return on $905,040, then your income is $45,252 a year. Is that enough to live on? What happens when your return is only 2%? Can you really live on $18,100 a year? Have you planned for a negative return? It does happen with mutual funds. What do you do then? How much can you withdraw and keep the nest egg large enough?

It is entirely possible to spend $1 million dollars in 12 years of retirement, depending on where you live and your current spending habits. The average life expectancy today is around 85 years and the average retirement age is 63 years, so where is the money coming from for the last 10 years of your life?

A lot of people, when they retire have their house paid off, but a lot don't. You still have taxes to pay, both on your house and the income you are drawing on, which happens with a Traditional IRA. If you go with a Roth IRA, you pay taxes on your investments in the beginning and no tax is paid when you start withdrawing, which is a much better arrangement for you.

Are you paying rent? That figure will never be lower than it is today. Food bills will remain the same unless you plan on eating only once or twice a day. Gas and electricity charges will be at least what you are paying now, probably more since you are not working in another location any more. You will still probably have cable, internet and phone bills to pay and I haven't even mentioned inflation. Can you really live on less than half of what you are currently making? What is your quality of life going to be like?

I ask you these questions to encourage you to think, not to depress you. If you take charge now, then life is much better in retirement. You may be saying, "I'm okay, I have money invested in a mutual fund". How much is in the account? Do you have any control over what they are investing in? What fees are you paying? Do you know what risks they are taking with your money? How do you know that there will be enough in the account when you retire?

Very few people in the finance industry will have your best interests at heart and even less will be able to manage your money better than you can. They say they want to do what is best for you, but then lobby the Government to pass laws that benefit them, not you.

Did you know that 96% of mutual and hedge fund managers

can't even beat the S&P 500? And the ones that do aren't the same ones every year. They also charge outrageous fees that eat into your retirement income (see chapter three for full details).

According to retirement plan provider, Fidelity Investments, you should have 10 times your final salary in savings at retirement. But that is only $603,660 according to the median salary. They also suggest that you should use the following timeline to be able to get to that magic number:

- Have the equivalent of your salary saved at age 30
- Have three times your salary saved at age 40
- Have six times your salary saved at age 50
- Have eight times your salary saved at age 60
- Have ten times your salary saved at age 67

These numbers are completely unobtainable for most people and are typical of the "investment advice" you will receive from finance professionals. Who has been able to save the equivalent of their salary at age 30? I don't know anyone that has ever been able to do that, particularly since most people with a degree are paying off a student loan and are typically on an entry level position.

You have so many things stacked against you by an industry that is designed to part you from your money. The average returns of most mutual funds and hedge funds are terrible, and they get paid whether you make money or not. You take all the risk and they take a substantial portion of your profits and are not exposed to any losses themselves. They speculate with your money and generally make bad investment decisions.

Now is the time to take charge of your financial future. If you keep doing what you are doing, you will just get the same results. Find someone who is older than you and has followed the same financial path that you are currently on. How are they coping as they approach retirement? Do they even have a plan?

Investing is not hard. You don't have to be a genius. But it does take time and if you wait 10 or 15 years before you start, then it is much more difficult to succeed. My investment principles are very simple and have a long-term approach grounded on the financial data of the companies I invest in. Most importantly, it is designed to protect your investment money at all costs.

CHAPTER TWO

The Dangers of Other People's Opinions

There are many voices and opinions in the financial world, most of which are not worth listening to. All analysts and financial experts that provide an opinion are paid to provide their opinion, whether it is accurate or not.

The fact is, no-one knows what the market will do. There are certain factors that can affect the market, such as a change in interest rates, world war, or a financial crisis in another part of the world. However, no-one can predict with absolute certainty what the market will do over any given time frame, a day, a year or a decade.

I have heard many opinions of so called "experts" over the

years. These people preach their theories as though they are fact and use fear and greed to motivate people to do what is best for them, not what's best for you. Do yourself a favor and stop listening to other people's financial opinions, even those with impressive credentials.

It is far better to develop your own opinion and really educate yourself rather than relying on others. Of course, we are taught to immediately trust someone in a position of authority such as a doctor, dentist or lawyer and these professionals are worthy of our trust for the most part.

However, this is not the case in the financial world. In fact, most finance professionals are either guessing, or pushing their company's financial products for a large commission. They may say (and even believe) that they have your best interests at heart, but they really don't. Their job is to make as much money from you as possible in the form of fees. Chapter three goes into full detail of the fees you are currently paying.

Where are you getting your investment advice? If you're like most people, it is probably from journalists that write for The Wall Street Journal, Forbes, Money Magazine, New York Times, The Economist or something similar. Or, you could be speaking with a registered Financial Advisor. Surely a registered Financial Advisor has the right answers, right? Well, sadly they don't.

So, how much are these professionals getting paid for their advice? They certainly have some impressive titles. What makes them worth listening to? Here's a rundown of investment professional annual salaries (in USD) according to Glassdoor. The figures will surprise you.

Position	Median Pay
Financial Advisor	$47K
Financial Advisor Associate	$52K
Financial Analyst	$72K
Financial Planner	$57K
Financial Representative	$47K
Investment Consultant	$61K

Not very impressive. None of these people make more than $100,000 a year. Would you really trust them for investment advice?

How about the people that actively manage your money through trading stocks, bonds and options? Surely, they must be paid a lot, right? Again, the results are surprising.

Position	Median Pay
Mutual Fund Manager	$95K
Hedge Fund Manager	$110K
Hedge Fund Analyst	$70K
Private Equity Analyst	$82K
Equity Analyst	$99K
Equity Research Analyst	$97K
Investment Analyst	$95K
Mutual Fund Analyst	$71K

Equally unimpressive. Did you notice the median salaries for the Mutual and Hedge Fund Managers? These are the people that are actively making the investment decisions when they manage your money. Surely, they should be paid much more for their incredible investment knowledge. Aren't they the "experts"?

Does anyone know what investment guidelines or processes the mutual fund managers and hedge fund managers are following? Are they accountable for bad decisions? Unfortunately, they are not accountable and can make any decision they choose to, based on the underlying charter of the fund. If they want to pay an outrageous stock price for Google (GOOG), IBM (IBM) or Facebook (FB), they can (and often do).

What about your investment advisor? Remember, their median salary is just $47,000 a year. To be able to give investment advice for compensation, your advisor must pass the Series 65 exam to become a Registered Investment Advisor (RIA). The exam takes around 3 hours to do and focuses primarily on the responsibilities of the RIA when they start managing money or giving investment advice. There is nothing in there that makes them better investors.

The salaries for financial journalists are also lower than would be expected. According to Glassdoor, The Wall Street Journal pays their journalists between $54,000 and $107,000 a year with a median of $76,000. Forbes pays between $40,000 to $140,000 with a median of $53,000. The New York Times is a little better with salaries between $95,000 and $115,000 and a median of $106,000. The Economist is the worst of all with salaries between $42,000 and $78,000 with a median of $64,000.

The sad part is that all of these "professionals" are being trusted for their advice, really without question. Do you want to trust your financial future to a person that is quite probably paid less than you are? Ask them about their own investment portfolios and you will find that they probably don't even have one. If they do, they certainly won't show you how poorly they are doing.

CHAPTER THREE

What You Are Getting From Your Current Funds

Take a deep breath...

"The mutual fund industry is now the world's largest skimming operation, a $7 trillion trough from which fund managers, brokers, and other insiders are steadily siphoning off an excessive slice of the nation's household, college, and retirement savings."

> Sen. Peter Fitzgerald, composer of the mutual fund Reform Act of 2004 (killed by the Senate Banking Committee)

Financial news today is a lot more entertainment and sensationalism than it is "news". People will scream their hot picks of the day while sound effects, smash crash and "ka-ching" in the background. Reporters will film live from the trenches of the exchange room floor in a system which is paid for by advertisers to make us feel that we are missing out. If only we had the next hot tip or the next "must-own" mutual fund that is the next five-star raging success.

How can you tell what's false and what's true? Where do you put your money? Who can you trust? Usually, most people put their money in a mutual fund that is focused on the stock market. The stock market has indeed been the best long-term investment for the past 100 years. Steve Forbes says "$1 million invested in stocks in 1935 is worth $2.4 billion today (if you held on)".

So, people hand over their money to a five-star actively managed mutual fund manager who is trying to beat the market by being a better stock picker than everyone else. However, almost no one will tell you what is sometimes called the "$13 trillion lie".

An incredible 96% of actively managed mutual funds fail to beat the market (the S&P 500) over any sustained period of time.

SO MANY DIFFERENT MUTUAL FUNDS

Currently, there are 7,707 different mutual funds in the United States all competing for your money to help you "beat the market". It's interesting to note that there are only around 4,900 individual stocks. Of these 7,707 mutual funds, 96% of them will fail to match or beat the market over any extended period of time. To put that in perspective, less than 400 of the 7,707 different mutual funds will have a better return than the S&P 500.

Even Warren Buffett, who is known for his ability to find undervalued stocks, says that the average investor should never try to pick stocks or time the market. Ray Dalio of Bridgewater Associates says "You're not going to beat the market. No one does. Only a few gold medalists."

Warren Buffett is so sure of this that he made a $1 million wager in 2008 with New York-based Protégé Partners, with all winnings going to charity. What was the wager? Can Protégé pick five top hedge fund managers that will collectively beat the S&P 500 over a ten-year period. A hedge fund is essentially a private "closed door" fund for high net worth individuals, where the manager has total flexibility to buy or sell stocks as he sees fit.

The result? The S&P 500 won hands down with an average annual return of 7.1% per year while the five funds had an average annual return of only 2.2%.

FACTS ARE FACTS

Robert Arnott is an industry expert and founder of Research Affiliates. He spent two decades studying the top 200 actively managed mutual funds that have at least $100 million in assets under management. From 1984 to 1998, only eight of the 200 fund managers beat the Vanguard 500 index, which is an index put together by Jack Bogle that is a mirror image of the S&P 500 index.

That is a 4% chance of picking a winner. If you have ever played blackjack, you know that if you are dealt two face cards (each worth 10), you have an awesome hand. The goal of blackjack is to get as close to 21 as possible. If your "inner idiot" wants to get to 21, you have an 8% chance of being dealt an ace (worth 1 or 11) for the next card, which is a better chance of winning than picking the correct mutual fund.

Over a 20-year period, from December 31, 1993 to December 31, 2013 the S&P 500 returned an average annual return of 9.28%, but the average mutual fund investor made just over 2.54% in the same time, according to Dalbar, one of the leading industry research firms. That is nearly an 80% difference. When I back tested my approach during the same time period using stocks from the S&P 500, I achieved an average annual return of 10.20%.

If you simply owned the SPDR® S&P 500® ETF (SPY), you would have turned $10,000 into $55,916. But, if you were a typical mutual fund investor, sold on the illusion that your fund manager will beat the market, you would have ended up with only $16,386.

Why? Because most investors buy high and sell low. They follow their emotions (or the recommendations of their broker) and jump from fund to fund always looking for the edge. When the market falls, they can't take the emotional pain any longer and sell. When the market rises, they buy.

A HARSH REALITY

You might be thinking that there must be some people who can beat the market. Why else would there be $13 trillion in actively managed mutual funds? Mutual fund managers do have streaks where they do beat the market, but they can't sustain it over time. As Jack Bogle said, "It all comes down to marketing". Selling a hot fund is not difficult to do because everybody wants to be part of it. That hot fund will inevitably turn cold and when it does there is another fund ready to serve.

What about the 4% that do beat the market? Well, most of the time they are not the same 4% the next time around. According to Jack Bogle, "If you pack 1,024 gorillas into the gymnasium and teach them each to flip a coin, one of them will flip heads 10 times in a row. Most would call that luck, but when that happens in the fund business we call him a genius." What are the odds that the same guerrilla would do it again?

Some mutual fund managers will say that they may not outperform on the upside, but when the market goes down they take active measures to protect their clients' money so that they don't lose much. This would be comforting if it were actually true.

In 2008 and early 2009, the stock market had its worst one-year slide since the Great Depression (51% top to bottom). The mutual fund managers had plenty of time to make their defensive moves. Maybe when the market was down 15%, or 25%, or even 35% they could have taken "appropriate measures". But they didn't, and millions of people lost everything.

Whether these fund managers were trying to beat the S&P 500 Growth Index, or the S&P Small Cap index, these fund managers fell way short of the mark. According to a 2012 report called S&P Indices Versus Active Funds Scorecard, the S&P 500 Growth Index outperformed 89.9% of large-cap growth mutual funds, while the S&P 500 Small Cap growth index outperformed 95.5% of small-cap growth manages.

THE UNICORNS – THOSE THAT ACTUALLY CAN BEAT THE MARKET

There is a tiny group of hedge fund managers who consistently beat the market. These are the unicorns, the rarest of the rare. People like David Einhorn of Greenlight Capital, who is up 2,287% since launching his fund in 1996 with only one negative year. Unfortunately, his doors are closed to new investors. Or Ray Dalio, who founded Bridgewater Associates, hasn't accepted new investors for at least 10 years, but when they were accepting investors it required a minimum investment of $100 million and $5 billion in investable assets.

For the 5th year in a row, ending in 2012, the vast majority of hedge fund managers underperformed the S&P 500. According to Zero Hedge, financial news site, in 2012 the average fund returned 8% compared with 16% for the S&P 500. In 2013, hedge funds returned an average of 7.4% while the S&P 500 soared to 29.6%, which was its best year since 1997.

To make it worse, these hedge fund managers usually charge 2% per year for management, take 20% of the overall profits, and the gains you receive are often taxed at the highest tax rates.

IT PAYS TO BE A STAR

According to Morningstar, for the decade ending in December 2009, roughly 72% of all fund deposits (about $2 trillion) went to four and five-star funds. Morningstar evaluates mutual funds and applies a five-star rating system to their past performance. Brokers will always share with you the next hot fund rated by Morningstar.

David Swenson, chief investment officer of Yale University, says "The stars are so important that mutual fund companies are quick to eliminate funds which fall below the four-star threshold. For the five-year period ending in 2012, 27% of domestic equity funds and 23% of international equity funds were either merged or liquidated; a common practice to eliminate a poor track record from a family of funds."

It's common practice for mutual fund companies to set up multiple funds at once and see which one is hot, then killing the others. Jack Bogle explains "A firm will go out and start five incubation funds, and they will try and shoot the lights out with all five of them. And of course, they don't with four of them, but they do with one. So, they drop the other four and take the one that did very well public with a great track record and sell that track record".

In an article from the Wall Street Journal called *Investors Caught With Stars In Their Eyes*, researchers went back to 1999 and studied the 10 year subsequent performance of those who bought five-star funds. Of the 248 mutual stock funds with a five-star rating at the start, only four kept the five-star rating after 10 years. In effect, you have a 98% chance of your investment fizzling out to nothing. History tells us that the hot fund will turn cold.

FEES ON FEES

Very few people know how much they pay mutual fund

management companies in fees. In fact, these companies have become experts at either hiding their fees or convincing you that the fees are not important and "no big deal". Nothing could be further from the truth. You can't afford to take two steps forward and one step back by letting excessive fees drain your account. Are you funding your retirement or someone else's?

FINE PRINT

The $13 trillion mutual fund industry uses fine print to hide their outrageous fees. In the Forbes article *The Real Cost Of Owning A Mutual Fund,* Ty Bernicke demonstrates the actual costs of owning a mutual fund. The actual cost is 3.17% per year according to Ty.

Now if you were able to invest with Ray Dalio of Bridgewater Associates, who has a reported 21% annualized return (before fees) since launching his fund, 3.17% would be worth it. Unfortunately, Ray Dalio no longer accepts clients.

1% HERE 1% THERE

"Just" 1% here, 1% there. It doesn't sound like a whole lot but compounded over time, it will be the difference between your money lasting your entire life or being forced to find other ways to fund your retirement such as government assistance or going back to work at Walmart or Kroger.

If you have $100,000 to invest at the market rate of 7% annually and leave it for 30 years, your balance will be vastly different depending on whether you are charged 3%, 2%, or 1% in fees. If you are charged 3% in annual fees, your total after 30 years is $324,340. For 2% in annual fees, after 30 years your total is $432,194. If you're fortunate enough to only pay 1% in annual fees, your total is $574,349, which is $250,009 more money in your account than if you had paid 3% in annual fees.

Now granted this is a hypothetical example, so let's get real. Between January 1, 2000 and December 31, 2012, the S&P 500 was flat and had an average annual return of 1.54%. This time period is often referred to as the lost decade because most people made no progress at all and had to endure massive volatility with the run-up through 2007, the free-fall drop in 2008, and the bull market run that began in 2009. My investment approach returned 8.28% during the same period when I back tested using stocks in the S&P 500.

Let's say that $100,000 was your life savings and if you simply owned or "mimicked" the market during this period your account was flat, and your fees were minimal. But if you had paid the 3.17% in average annual fees, assuming your fund manager could even match the market, you would pay over $30,000 in fees. Your account was down nearly 30% (around $70,000 left), but the market was flat. You would have put up all the capital, taking all the risk, but your fund manager would have made over $30,000.

Mutual fund companies use misdirection to get you to focus on something else while they subtly remove your watch. The expense ratio is the "sticker price" that is most commonly reported in their marketing materials, but it doesn't tell the whole story.

PhD IN FEES

Just after the 2008 crash, Robert Hiltonsmith graduated with a PhD in economics, got a job and started making contributions to his 401(k). He noticed that even though the market was rising, his account would rarely rise with it. He decided to take it on as a research project is started by reading the 50+ page prospectus of each of the 20 funds he had invested in. This literature is incredibly boring and dry legalese which was designed to be "very opaque" according to Hiltonsmith.

There was language that he couldn't understand, many acronyms, and most importantly a catalog of 17 different fees that he was being charged. There were also additional costs that were not actually direct fees but were being paid for by the investors in all the funds.

Wall Street, and the vast majority of 401(k) plan providers, have come up with some pretty diverse and confusing terminology to better hide their fees. Here are just some of them: asset management 12b-1 fees, marketing fees, trading costs (brokerage commissions, spread costs, market impact costs), soft-dollar costs, redemption fees, account fees, purchase fees, record-keeping fees, plan administrative fees, and so on. All these fees cost you money.

After over a month of research, Hiltonsmith concluded that his 401(k) could not flourish with all these excessive and hidden fees. In his report, titled *The Retirement Savings Drain: The Hidden & Excessive Costs of 401(k)s*, he calculated that the average worker will lose $154,794 to 401(k) fees over their lifetime, which is based on an annual income of around $30,000 per year and a savings plan of 5% per year. A higher income worker, who makes around $90,000 per year, will lose over $277,000 in fees in their lifetime.

David Swenson, who is the chief investment officer of Yale's endowment, and managed to turn $1 billion into $23.9 billion states "Overwhelmingly, mutual funds extract enormous sums from investors in exchange for providing a shocking disservice."

Actively managed mutual funds are heavily marketed and for the most part, are part of a disastrous social experiment that began with the advent of the 401(k) in the early 80s. The 401(k) was only meant to be a supplement to a traditional pension plan and was a good idea for those that wanted to put extra money away. Today there is over $13 trillion in managed mutual funds, most of which is held in retirement accounts such as 401(k) and IRAs.

Not only do they rarely beat the market, but most charge astronomical fees for their mediocrity. The fees will cost tens of millions of people their quality of life in their retirement and are the number one danger and destroyer of financial freedom. Jack Bogle, the founder of Vanguard says, "I think high costs (eroding already lower returns) are as much of a risk for investors as the economic situation in Europe or China."

IT GETS WORSE

Let's recap. The vast majority (96%) of actively managed mutual funds cannot beat the market and charge you excessive fees that extract up to two thirds of your potential nest egg. But that's not the worst part - they will look you in the eye and tell you that they truly have your best interests at heart while simultaneously lobbying Congress to make sure that is never the case.

The average plan administrator charges between 1.3% to 1.5% annually just to participate in the 401(k) (according to the Government Accountability Office) and that's not counting the other hidden fees. When you add this 1.3% for the plan administration to the total mutual fund costs of 3.17%, it can be more expensive to own a fund in a tax-free account when compared with the taxable account (4.47% to 4.67% per year).

To escape the fee factories, you must lower your total annual fees and associated investment costs to 1.25% or less. This means the cost of the advice and the cost of investments should be 1.25% or less.

BREAKDOWN OF FEES

Expense Ratio

The expense ratio is the number that they want you to focus on. According to Morningstar, US stock funds pay an average of 1.31% to the fund company for portfolio management and operating expenses such as marketing (12-b-1 fees), distribution and administration. Many of the larger funds have realized that a 1% expense ratio is where they want to be at and investors don't generally object to the fee.

Transaction Costs

Transaction costs are a broad category that can be broken down into further categories such as brokerage commissions, market impact costs and spread costs. A study conducted in 2006 by business school professors Roger Edelen, Richard Evans, and Gregory Kadlec found that US stock mutual funds average 1.44% in transaction costs per year. These transaction costs are the most expensive part of owning a mutual fund, but the industry has deemed it too difficult to quantify and it is unreported in the brochures.

Tax Costs (or 401(k) costs)

Many people are excited about the so-called "tax-deferred" treatment of their 401(k), but for most employees, the tax cost has been swapped out with "plan administrative" fees. These "plan administrative" fees are charged in addition to the fees paid to the underlying mutual funds, and according to the Government Accountability Office, the average plan administrator charges 1.13% per year. If you own a mutual fund in a taxable account, the average tax cost is between 1.0% and 1.2% annually, according to Morningstar.

Soft-Dollar Costs

Soft-dollar trading is an arrangement whereby mutual fund managers pay inflated trading costs so that the outside firm executing the trades will then rebate the additional cost back to the fund manager. It's a rewards program for using a particular vendor. The fund manager can use these funds to pay for expenses such as research and reports, which are costs the fund manager would otherwise have to pay. These costs are unreported and impossible to quantify.

Cash Drag

Mutual fund managers must maintain a cash position to provide daily liquidity and satisfy any selling redemptions. Since this cash is not invested, it doesn't generate a return. According to a study titled *Dealing With The Active* by William O'Reilly (CFA) and Michael Preisano (CFA), the average cost from cash drag on large-cap stock mutual funds over 10 years is 0.83% per year.

Redemption Fee

If you want to sell your fund position, you must pay a redemption fee, which is paid to the fund company directly. The US Securities and Exchange Commission (SEC) limits the redemption fee to 2%. Just like the world's most expensive ATM, it will cost you $2,000 to get your $100,000 back.

Exchange Fee

Many funds charge a fee to move or exchange from one fund to another within the same family of funds.

Account Fee

Many funds charge you a maintenance fee just to have an account.

Purchase Fee

A purchase fee (different from a front-end sales commission) is charged to purchase the fund and goes directly to the fund company.

Sales Charge (Load) or Deferred Sales Charge

This charge is paid to a broker and comes out when you purchase the fund (so a smaller amount of your initial deposit is used to buy shares in the fund), or you pay the charge when you exit the fund and redeem your shares.

HEDGE FUND RETURNS – WHAT YOU SEE IS NOT WHAT YOU GET

"Surprise, the returns reported by mutual funds aren't actually earned by investors."

Jack Bogle, founder of Vanguard

"Most people are familiar with the boilerplate disclaimer that past performance doesn't guarantee future results. Far fewer are aware of how past performance numbers themselves can be misleading."

How Funds Massage Numbers, Legally Wall Street Journal, March 31, 2013

THE MARKET IS NOT WHAT IT SEEMS

Let's say the market is up and down like a roller coaster, which does happen. Up 50%, down 50%, up 50% again and then down 50% again. This produces an average return of 0%. But don't expect that a 0% return means you don't lose money. The table below illustrates my point.

Initial Investment	50% Up	50% Down	50% Up	50% Down
$100,000	$150,000	$75,000	$112,500	$56,250

In this scenario, with an initial investment of $100,000 and the market behaving like a roller coaster, you would have lost $43,750 or 43.75% of your portfolio.

In an article by Erik Krom of Fox Business called *Solving The Myth of Rate of Return*, Erik explains how this applies to the real world. "Another way to look at it is to review the Dow Jones since 1930. If you add up every number and divide it by 81 years the return 'averages' 6.31%; however, if you do the math, you get an 'actual' return of 4.31%. Why is this so important? If you invested $1,000 back in 1930 at 6.31%, you would have $142,000, at 4.31% you would only have $30,000."

THE SCALES ARE WEIGHTED

When a mutual fund advertises a return, it is often not the return you get. The returns you see in the brochures are known as time-weighted returns.

If the fund has $1 at the beginning of the year and $1.20 at the end of the year, the fund manager will claim that he has made a 20% return and the marketing department will start churning out the ads. But investors rarely have all their money in the fund at the beginning of the year and typically make contributions throughout the year, especially if they have a 401(k).

If an investor contributes more during times when the fund is performing well, which is quite common because people chase returns, and less during times when the fund is not performing, that investor will have a much different return from what is advertised.

TIME-WEIGHTED RETURNS AND DOLLAR-WEIGHTED RETURNS

If that same investor sat down at the end of the year, and analyzed their ongoing contributions and withdrawals, they would find out how much they really made or lost. This real-world approach is called the dollar-weighted return. The dollar-weighted return is the return you get to keep, but time-weighted returns are the returns that fund managers use to fuel their advertising.

Jack Bogle, the founder of Vanguard says: "We've compared returns earned by mutual fund investments; dollar-weighted returns, with the returns earned by the fund themselves, or time-weighted returns, and the investors seem to lag the fund themselves by 3% per year." This means that if a fund advertises a 6% return, its investors achieved closer to 3%.

Don't believe what the fund managers (also known as salesman or brokers) and the glossy brochures are telling you. The truth is that you're being misled, and it is being done intentionally.

YOUR BROKER IS NOT YOUR FRIEND

" It's difficult to get a man to understand something, when
his salary depends on his not understanding it."
Upton Sinclair

Your broker will look at you with sincerity and tell you that he has your best interests at heart. He's either lying or misinformed. Sometimes he genuinely believes he is helping you based on the information that he has.

As a financial services representative, your broker should be giving you the best advice that is available. The reality is, he gets paid to give you the advice that benefits his company, not you. In the face of a constant barrage of conflicting information and marketing hype, people become quickly overwhelmed and "hope" becomes their strategy.

This current run from 2009 is one of the longest in history. People are seeing their account balances rise again and are starting to feel comfortable. Mutual fund managers and executives are raking it in, but the sharks are still feeding.

PROTECTION FROM WHOM?

In 2009, Representatives Barney Frank and Chris Dodd submitted a proposed regulation called the *Dodd-Frank Wall Street Reform and Consumer Protection Act*. A year later, following extensive lobbying by the financial services community, a version of the bill passed with far less teeth than the original. The question is, from whom or what do we need protection from? From the people we trust to manage our finances? From the managers themselves who legally line their pockets? From the high-frequency traders who steal millions of dollars, one penny at a time?

Just recently we have seen rogue traders cause billions in losses for banks. Large firms such as MF Global misappropriated client funds and then declared bankruptcy. There have been insider-trading convictions from one of the world's largest hedge funds. Bank traders have been criminally prosecuted for rigging LIBOR

(London Interbank Offered Rates), the world's benchmark for short-term interest rates.

FUND MANAGERS RARELY INVEST IN THEIR OWN FUNDS

In a study released by Morningtar in 2009 which tracked over 4,300 actively managed mutual funds, they showed that 49% of the managers did not own any shares in the fund they manage. That's right, the chef doesn't eat his own food.

Of the remaining 51%, most own only a token amount of their funds in comparison with their total net worth. To summarize:

- 2,126 managers don't own any shares in the fund they manage
- 159 managers invested between $1 and $10,000 in their own fund
- 393 managers invested between $10,001 and $50,000
- 285 managers invested between $50,001 and $500,000
- 679 managers invested between $100,001 and $500,000
- 197 managers invested between $500,001 and $999,999
- 413 managers invested more than $1 million

Are your interests aligned? Does your broker or finance professional have every incentive to operate in your best interests? Sadly, the answer is no. David Swenson, head of Yale University's $23 billion fund, says "Your broker is not your friend".

THE SUITABILITY STANDARD

The financial services industry has many people who want to do what's in the best interest of their clients, but many are operating in an environment where the financial tools available to them are in the best interests of their company. This system rewards them for selling, not for providing conflict free advice. The fund that they sell you does not have to be the best available, or even in your best interests. All it's required to be is "suitable". Their legal requirement is to provide you with the product that is classified as suitable.

According to David Karp, a registered investment advisor, the standard suitability is as follows: "It doesn't matter who benefits more, the client or advisor. As long as an investment is suitable (meets the general direction of your goals and objectives) at the time it was placed for the client, the advisor is held free of liability."

Most people don't know if their investment professional is a broker or legal fiduciary and almost everybody believes that their investment professional should have their best interest at heart. Since these people are operating within a framework that rewards them for selling, it is impossible for them to have your best interests at heart.

You will never hear these people referred to as "brokers". Instead they are called registered representatives, financial advisors, wealth advisors, vice presidents of this or that. The Wall Street Journal has reported finding over 200 different professional designations for financial advisors and more than half are not tracked by the Financial Industry Regulatory Authority (FINRA), which oversees how investments are pitched to investors.

E N R O N

Remember Enron? They were an energy giant with $101 billion in annual revenue in 2000. They decided to doctor the books in hopes of keeping shareholders happy. There were many big brokers and mutual funds that owned most of the Enron shares and were big fans of the company.

In March 2001, nine months after declaring bankruptcy, Enron signaled that it was having trouble. Anybody who looked at the cash flow statement could see that they were fast losing cash. But this didn't stop the big Wall Street firms from recommending the stock.

If you look at the following table, you'll see that the recommendation to buy or hold was made until there was nothing left to hold because the stock had no value and the company was bankrupt.

Date	Recommendation	Stock Price	Company
Mar 21, 2001	"Near Term Buy"	$55.89	Merrill Lynch
Mar 29, 2001	"Recommended List"	$55.31	Goldman Sachs
Jun 8, 2001	"Buy"	$47.26	J.P. Morgan
Aug 15, 2001	"Strong Buy"	$40.25	Bank of America
Oct 4, 2001	"Buy"	$33.10	AG Edwards
Oct 24, 2001	"Strong Buy"	$16.41	Lehman Brothers
Nov 12, 2001	"Hold"	$9.24	Prudential
Nov 21, 2001	"Market Perform"	$5.01	Goldman Sachs
Nov 29, 2001	"Hold"	$0.36	Credit Suisse First
Dec 2, 2001	Bankrupt	$0.00	

401(k)

"Baby boomers have been the primary mice used in the great 401(k) retirement experiment."

Doug Warren, author of The Synergy Effect

The 401(k) is a terrific piece of tax code that, when used correctly, will power your retirement for years to come. But when it is used as it is in most plans, it will damage your chances for financial freedom.

401(k) HISTORY

The 401(k) was given to us in 1984 and allowed average Americans to participate in the stock market. It also allowed us to save on our taxes by making tax-deductible contributions from our paychecks. But the 401(k) was never meant to be the only retirement plan for us.

According to John Shoven, a professor of economics at Stanford, he says "you can't save just 3% of your income for 30 years and expect to live another 30 years in retirement with the same income you had when you were working."

The 401(k) social experiment is only a few decades old and we're now seeing a generation where the majority will retire having only used a 401(k) during their lifetime.

As we look back in history, the 401(k), which started out as a loophole for highly paid executives to put away cash, emerged as a boon for companies to eliminate the cost and obligation of traditional pensions and shift all the risk and expense to the employees. At the time, employees were quite willing to take on this new responsibility because stocks were soaring, and money flowed into the stock market like never before.

All that new money deposited into the stock market meant lots of buying, which fueled the bull markets of the 80s and 90s. There were trillions up for grabs and mutual fund companies began an unprecedented war to manage your money. The stock market changed from being a place where companies turned to the public to exchange cash ownership (primarily high net worth individuals) to a place where life savings were regularly invested by everyday Americans.

AN ILLUSION OF CONTROL

The 401(k) represented freedom and freedom often gives us the illusion of control. When markets rise we often mistake luck for being a "good investor".

According to Dr. Alicia Munnell, director of the Center For Retirement Research at Boston College, she says "We went from a system of defined benefits - where people had a pension; they had an income for life - to the idea of the 401(k), which was obviously cheaper for employers. And on the surface, it seemed like it was beneficial to individuals because they had more control of their own investment decisions."

Teresa Ghilarducci of the New School for Social Research puts it quite well in her article in the New York Times titled *Our Ridiculous Approach To Retirement*:

"Not yet convinced that failure is backed into the voluntary, self-directed, commercially run retirement plans system? Consider what would have to happen for it to work for you. First, figure out when you and your spouse will be laid off or be too sick to work. Second, figure out when you will die. Third, understand that you need to save 7% of every dollar you earn. (Didn't start doing that when you were 25, and you are 55 now? Just save 30% of every dollar) Fourth, earn at least 3% above inflation on your investments, every year. (Easy. Just find the best funds for the lowest price and have them optimally allocated). Fifth, do not withdraw any funds when you lose your job, have a health problem, get divorced, buy a house, or send a kid to college. Sixth, time your retirement account withdrawals so the last cent is spent the day you die."

To recap, actively managed stock-picking mutual funds rarely beat the market, which is exactly what you find in the vast majority of 401(k) plans. These expensive funds charge outrageous fees eroding 50% to 70% of our retirement nest egg.

Now when you stick those mutual funds inside a name brand 401(k) plan, offered by a payroll or insurance company, you will be charged a range of additional costs as follows:

Communication expenses
- Enrollment materials
- Ongoing materials
- Enrollment meetings
- Investment advice

Record-keeping and administrative expenses
- Base fee

- Per participant fee
- Per eligible employee fee
- Distribution
- Loan origination
- Loans maintenance
- Semiannual discrimination testing
- 5500 filing package
- Other expenses

Investment expenses
- Base fee
- Individual mutual fund expenses
- Manager/advisor fee
- Other asset fees (revenue-sharing, wrap, administration)

Trustee expenses
- Base fee
- Per participant fee
- Asset charge

One industry insider called his own industry "the largest dark pool of assets when nobody really knows how or whose hands are getting greased". The 401(k) industry has been around for decades, but it was only in 2012 that service providers become required by law to disclose fees on statements. Even with the disclosure, more than half of all employees have no idea how much that they are paying. In fact, according to a 2011 study called *401(k) Participants' Awareness and Understanding of Fees* by AARP, 71%, of people enrolled in 401(k)s think that there are no fees.

Did you know that the owner of any company is also the plan sponsor and has a legal duty to make sure that his employees are not taken advantage of?

Would it surprise you that the so-called choices on the 401(k) plan are not the best choices available? They're the ones that pay the most to be offered up on the list of available funds. So how do they recoup their costs to be on the list? High fees. Consequently, you are failing to get the best performing funds and you're paying higher fees for inferior performance.

This chapter is based on the ground-breaking work of Tony Robbins in his book Money, Master The Game.

CHAPTER FOUR

Which Companies to Invest In

The number one reason people fail in the Stock Market is by buying stocks in the wrong companies. There is a vast array of choices available.

Currently, there are 2,659 companies listed on the New York Stock Exchange (NYSE) under 3,142 stock symbols, 3,439 companies listed on the National Association of Securities Dealers Automated Quotations (NASDAQ) and 326 companies listed on NYSE American (formerly known as AMEX). These are just the American exchanges. Some of the foreign exchanges include Japan Exchange Group, Shanghai Stock Exchange, Euronext, London Stock Exchange Group, Hong Kong Stock Exchange, Shenzhen Stock Exchange, Deutsche Borse, Bombay Stock Exchange, National Stock Exchange of India,

TMX Group, Korea Exchange, SIX Swiss Exchange, NASDAQ Nordic, Australian Securities Exchange, JSE Limited, Taiwan Stock Exchange, B3 and BME Spanish Exchanges. That's a long list and that is not even all the world's registered stock exchanges!

What about Hedge Funds and Mutual Funds? At the time of this writing, there are 61,057 entries registered on the Securities and Exchange Commission with the word "fund" in their name. There are too many choices available for anyone to make an informed decision as to what to invest in.

MID CAP, LARGE CAP AND MEGA CAP COMPANIES LISTED ON THE NYSE

I invest in companies that are in any of the following categories on the New York Stock Exchange (NSYE):

- Mid Cap (companies with a market capitalization of between $2 billion and $10 billion)
- Large Cap (companies with a market capitalization of between $10 billion and $200 billion)
- Mega Cap (companies with a market capitalization of greater than $200 billion)

You can get the list of Mid Cap, Large Cap and Mega Cap companies from the following URL on the NASDAQ site:
https://www.nasdaq.com/screening/companies-by-industry.aspx
Look to the menu on the left and scroll down to see the links.

None of the companies on the Mid Cap, Large Cap or Mega Cap lists are likely to go out of business any time soon, particularly for Large Cap and Mega Cap companies. Mid Cap companies are still quite safe, although the risk is a little higher. It is a matter of balancing risk versus reward.

Investing in these companies will protect you from a company going bankrupt. If a company files Chapter 11 bankruptcy, you will more than likely lose all your money and your stocks will be worthless. Just ask anyone who had the misfortune of owning Enron shares in 2001.

S & P 5 0 0

If your risk tolerance is low, then you could limit your investments to companies that are in the current list of the S&P 500. These companies can survive the next major market crash without going bankrupt. Your returns will be a little lower than if you include Mid Cap companies, but you will still beat the S&P 500 using my investment approach. I back tested my approach to 1993 with stocks in the S&P 500 and my average annual return was 9.44% compared with the average annual return of 8.44% for the S&P 500 for the same time period.

The S&P 500 is regarded by the financial world as the best single gauge of large-cap U.S. companies and is what is commonly referred to as "the market". When you hear the talking heads talking about "the market", they are referring to the S&P 500. The index includes 500 of the largest companies in the US, controls around 80% of the available market, and is a very good representation of the US economy.

To make the S&P 500, companies must meet the following criteria according to Standard & Poor as follows:

- **Universe.** All constituents must be U.S. companies
- **Eligibility Market Cap.** Companies with market cap of USD 6.1 billion or greater.
- **Public Float.** At least 50% of shares outstanding must be available for trading.
- **Financial Viability.** Companies must have positive as-reported earnings over the most recent quarter, as well as over the most recent four quarters (summed together).
- **Adequate Liquidity and Reasonable Price.** Consists of highly tradable common stocks, with active and deep markets.

THE DIVIDEND

In addition to making the list of companies on the Mid Cap, Large Cap or Mega Cap on the NYSE (or the S&P 500), the company must also pay a regular dividend with a long history of payment to make my watch list. There are currently 940 companies that are in the Mid Cap, Large Cap or Mega Cap lists that pay a dividend and 410 companies that pay a dividend in the S&P 500 at the time of this writing. The dividend is a share of the profits that a company pays at regular intervals, usually every quarter (3 months).

The dividend will allow you to sleep at night. I use the dividend to protect myself from making stupid or irrational sell decisions.

When you buy stock in a company that pays a regular dividend, the company will pay you a small amount per share every quarter. This payment is paid directly into your trading account and can be used to buy more shares in the company under the Dividend Reinvestment Programs (DRIPs) without having to pay another brokerage fee (typically ranging from $4.95 to $6.95 depending on the brokerage firm). Most brokerage firms will do it for free if you request it.

However, I recommend against DRIPs and personally use the dividend to invest in times of stock market crash. You need available cash when the market crashes to take advantage of the incredible bargains that are everywhere, and the dividend is perfect for that.

The dividend is an income stream that is paid to you every quarter. That means that you are being paid for owning the stock and you get paid every quarter until you decide to sell.

Imagine this scenario – you just bought 10 shares in Apple (AAPL), but the next day, the price goes down. You're a little worried, but not too worried because after all, it is Apple. But how do you feel 3 months later when the share price has lost 20% or even 50% of its value? It happens.

Share prices will often be lower or higher than they really should be and can plummet during times of market crash or soar to ridiculous levels based on the herd mentality of investors. The dividend will give you the peace of mind to be able to hold on to the stock even when the share price has dropped below what you paid for it. After all, it's paying you money. Why sell a stock at a loss when it is making you money?

In chapters five and seven, I will show you the right time to buy and sell your stock. Most people will buy and sell based upon what everyone else is doing, but this is a sure way to financial ruin. If you are doing what everyone else is doing, you will buy your stocks when they are too expensive and sell them for little or no profit.

NEVER LOSE MONEY

My number one rule is Never Lose Money. The consequences are high when you lose money and it is very easy to completely drain your investment account with a series of bad investment choices. It doesn't take much to have a losing year or even a series of losing years.

Just imagine you started your investment account with $100,000. It probably took a lot of discipline and effort to save that money and it would be very painful if you lost it. Most people start with a lot less than $100,000, but any loss is painful.

Let's take $100,000 as a starting point. In your first year, you lose 25%, bringing your account down to $75,000. Ouch! You tell yourself "It's okay, I'm just learning. I'll make it back next year."

Next year comes around and you are ready for it. It turns out that you had a pretty good year and make a 30% gain. So, you're back in profit and all is looking good. But year 3 rolls around and you make a 5% loss. No big deal, right? The next year, you make the 5% back in profit and you're ready to roll again. How much profit have you made on your initial $100,000 investment? Think about it for a moment.

Actually, you are over $2,700 in the red for a total of

$97,256.25 after 4 years of trading. What? How can that be! Your percentage gains were more than your losses. Unfortunately, your first year lost 25% of $100,000, which is $25,000. Your make up year of 30% was only on $75,000 for a total of $22,500.

	Start Amount	Gain / Loss	Balance
Year 1	$100,000	25% loss	$75,000
Year 2	$75,000	30% gain	$97,500
Year 3	$97,500	5% loss	$92,625
Year 4	$92,625	5% gain	$97,256.25

That's why it is so important to never lose money. It can take years to recover back to your starting point.

So, how do you not lose money? By buying stock that is paying a dividend and holding on to it until it is in profit. If the stock price drops, you have the confidence to hold on to it until the stock is in profit because it is paying you money every quarter.

You are in complete control over when you buy and when you sell. If there is a market crash, everyone else will panic and sell their stock, but you don't have to. Even if the market does crash, you can't make a loss if you don't sell your stock. The value of your portfolio will be down, but this value is based on what you would get for the stock if you sold right now, so it is meaningless. If you don't sell, you can wait for the market to recover and sell at the right time.

It is for this reason that you should never open an account on margin, which allows you to borrow money from the brokerage firm to buy more stock. Don't do it! When your account drops below a certain level, you will get a very unpleasant call from the broker telling you that you must deposit money into the account or they will sell your stock at a loss. Millions of people fell into this trap in the crash of 2008.

Holding on to a stock when the price is below what you bought it for is a mindset that you must master. It is a pure declaration of will that you refuse to lose, because every sale of a stock has a winner and a loser. Don't be the loser.

No-one can ever predict when a stock will do well, or when it will fall. There are indicators that will give you a fair idea, such as the Price to Earnings ratio (P/E), which I cover in chapters five and seven. I use the P/E to determine when I buy and sell. Often, when I buy a stock, the price will continue to drop because I am buying it based on the current financial data of the company, not the direction of the chart. The stocks I buy are out of favor with the market but are extremely well priced and have tremendous upside potential. Eventually, they become popular again and I sell them when everyone else is buying.

WHY YOU SHOULDN'T BUY STOCK WITHOUT A DIVIDEND

If you buy stock in a company such as Facebook (FB) or Google (GOOGL), both of which do not pay a dividend at the time of this writing, you will become obsessed about the stock and will get to the point where you are watching the charts every day.

If the stock price drops below what you paid for it, you will be able to handle it for a while, but there will come a time when your emotions will get the better of you. That's when you are most vulnerable. You think that you would never sell, but there will come a time when you will, particularly during a market correction or crash. Millions of people sold their stock at ridiculously low prices during the stock market crash of 2008.

The dividend is your protection from emotional irrationality and fear. The dividend is your downside protection.

CHAPTER FIVE

When To Buy

When you buy stock in a quality company that is in the Mid Cap, Large Cap, Mega Cap or S&P 500, you can be confident that the company won't go out of business. However, it is certainly possible to buy the stock at precisely the wrong time, which is what most people do when they follow the crowd. If a stock is popular, and everyone else is buying it, it must continue to keep going up right? Wrong!

By the time you hear about the hot tip, the stock has probably made its major move already and is ready to run out of gas and turn sharply on you. This is called regression to the mean in statistics, or a stock correction. It happens all the time.

The best time to buy a stock is when it is unpopular and few of the mutual funds or hedge funds are buying it. The only way to determine if a stock is a good buy or not is to use the Price to Earnings ratio (P/E).

THE PRICE TO EARNINGS RATIO (P/E)

I use the Price to Earnings ratio (P/E) to determine when I buy a stock. The P/E is very easy to calculate. You simply find the latest stock price for the stock you are interested in and divide it by the current earnings figure. The earnings figure is released each quarter by the company and is public record.

Let me show you an example for Apple (AAPL). The current price at the time of writing for Apple is $178.15, which you can find with a quick Google search. Finding the earnings figure is a little more difficult. You could go to their site and look for the latest Annual Report. Most companies in the Mid Cap, Large Cap and Mega Cap lists (or S&P 500) have an investor link on their site, usually at the bottom of the page. You can also search the Securities and Exchange Commission (SEC) website, or you can use a third part tool such as Morningstar, which is my preference. Most brokers also provide tools to be able to view the earnings.

If you look at the 2018 Annual Report for Apple, which you can find on the Apple website (apple.com), you will find current earnings on page 24. This is the same document that is recorded on the SEC databases and is available for anyone to download on the SEC website (sec.gov). You are looking for the Diluted Earnings Per Share, which is $11.91 for 2018.

The same figure of $11.91 is recorded on the Morningstar

website for the last 12 months (trailing twelve months or TTM) at the time of this writing, but this will change later. I prefer the TTM figure because it gives you a more accurate calculation. You certainly don't want to have earnings figures that are out of date by even a few months. You could work it out by some simple math calculations on the net income (minus the dividends) and the total shares outstanding, but the figures are already provided for you and they are accurate.

Back to calculating the P/E for Apple. The current price is $178.15, and the earnings figure is $11.91. The P/E is $178.15 divided by $11.91 = 14.95. This figure immediately tells me that Apple is a fairly good buy right now, but not good enough for me to buy their stock yet.

Let's calculate the P/E for Google. The current price for Google (GOOGL) is $1,087.55. The current earnings figure is $26.96. The P/E is $1,087.55 divided by $26.96 = 40.33. Remember that I would not buy Google stock until they start paying a regular dividend. However, if I did own Google stock, I would be selling right about now since it is becoming overpriced compared to what the company is actually earning, reflected in the Earnings Per Share (earnings) figure.

Try not to be alarmed at the price of the stock. Both Google and Apple are priced quite high, but both companies make a lot of money, which is reflected in the share price. Apple is currently priced slightly below what it should be, and Google is priced well above what would be considered a reasonable price.

Don't expect the market to price stock efficiently, even if the experts say that it does. Individual stock prices can be wildly unpredictable, and it is dangerous to try and predict where they are going next. You are looking for bargains based on what the company is earning, and bargains are available every trading day.

BUY WHEN THE PRICE TO EARNINGS (P/E) IS LESS THAN 10

The best time to buy a stock is when the P/E is less than 10. It means that the stock is extremely well priced compared to the rest of the market.

What is your favorite car? Just imagine that you could buy a brand-new Ferrari, Lamborghini, Maserati, Bugatti, BMW, Porsche, Mercedes Benz, Bentley, Aston Martin or Rolls Royce for the same price as a Toyota Camry or Chevy Cruze. You would jump at the chance. That's what is happening every trading day, you just have to be able to see it. All the companies in the Mid Cap, Large Cap, Mega Cap and S&P 500 are just like the list of cars I just mentioned. Each company in the S&P 500 is the best of the best and dominates its market share. There are approximately 30 – 50 stocks in the S&P 500 with a P/E of less than 10 every day and even more in the Mid Cap and Large Cap lists.

However, if the P/E is a negative number, do not buy the stock. This happens when the earnings are negative and that is a very bad sign. You would want to wait at least a year, preferably 2 or 3 to make sure that the company is still financially stable, particularly for stocks in the Mid Cap. A negative earnings figure may signal a significant fall in share price soon and may be the start of something much worse for the company. Companies like Nokia

(NOK) and Kodak (KODK) once dominated their respective industries and were in the S&P 500.

CHAPTER SIX

How To Set Up Your Portfolio

The first question you need to ask yourself is which broker to use. A broker is a company such as TD Ameritrade, Charles Schwab, E Trade and Ally Invest. These companies act as an intermediary between you and the market, allowing you to buy and sell stocks in exchange for a fee, usually between $4.95 and $6.95 per trade. The fee to trade is the same, whether you buy one stock or thousands of stocks at a time. These fees can really add up, which is why day trading is such a bad idea (more on that in chapter ten).

Each of the brokers below have their strengths and weaknesses. I prefer TD Ameritrade because of the features they provide. I really like the ability to export data in CSV format, which saves me a lot of time. Choose a broker that you can easily use and understand, because you don't want to be making mistakes when you buy and sell stocks.

Broker	Fees	Minimum	Website
TD Ameritrade	$6.95 per trade	$0	tdameritrade.com
Ally Invest	$4.95 per trade	$0	ally.com
E Trade	$6.95 per trade	$500	us.etrade.com
Merrill Edge	$6.95 per trade	$500	merrilledge.com
Trade Station	$5.00 per trade	$500	tradestation.com
Charles Schwab	$4.95 per trade	$0	schwab.com
Interactive Brokers	$0.01 per share	$0	interactivebrokers.com

If you are in another country, you can still open an account with most of these brokers. If you can't then there will be a good broker option available in your country. Ask other investors what they are using or do a Google search if all else fails.

When you open an account, make sure that you open the account with your own money, not a margin account. Margin is offered by almost all brokers and enables you to double your money by borrowing an equal amount. Half of the money belongs to the broker and they will expect a certain amount of money in the account to cover themselves from loss. Most people who open an account do it on margin and most of these people end up losing money.

When your account value drops below a certain amount (usually 30%), the broker will issue a margin call. If you receive a margin call, you will be required to deposit more money in the account or sell some of your existing stock. This can be very stressful if you don't have the money. If you don't have the money, the broker can legally sell your stock to cover themselves from loss.

They will sell your stock at a loss to cover themselves. Don't open an account with margin for any reason!

However, if you open an account with your money only, you never are forced to sell anything at a loss and you can hold the stock until it is in profit, which is the secret to keeping your account balance safe (and your sanity).

Each of the brokers listed previously will allow regular deposits from your bank account, allowing you to buy stocks on a regular basis. You can even set up a regular payment straight from your salary into your trading account. Speak to your HR department to set it up.

If the money is taken out of your paycheck before you see it, you won't be tempted to spend it on other things and you won't even miss it. Please make sure it is an amount that you can afford without putting any strain on your lifestyle. The money you set aside to invest will set you up for a comfortable life later and you really don't want to be spending it now.

ASSET ALLOCATION: HOW MANY STOCKS TO BUY

When you first set up an account, the number of stocks you buy initially will depend entirely on the amount of money in the account. If you have deposited $100,000 or more, then I recommend starting with between 40 – 50 stocks with a P/E of less than 10 if possible. Divide the money you have by the number of stocks you are going to buy so that you are spreading the money across the stocks evenly. For example, if you are going to buy 40 stocks, divide $100,000 by 40 = $2,500 to spend on each stock.

However, most people don't start with $100,000 in their account and often will set aside a certain amount each month to invest with. If you are starting with between $50,000 to $100,000 go for 30 stocks and if it is between $20,000 to $50,000 start with 20 stocks. For $10,000 to $20,000, go for 15 stocks.

The reality is that most people will start with far less than $10,000. You still want to maintain the balance on your portfolio because you need to protect yourself from buying only a few stocks. Diversification will protect you from any one company taking a huge loss that may take years to recover from. You don't want all your stock in one company.

If you have between $5,000 and $10,000 starting capital, then I recommend starting with 10 stocks. For between $2,000 and $5,000, go for between 5 - 8 stocks. For anything less than $2,000 you really have to start with a small portfolio of less than 5 stocks because fees then become an inhibiting factor and will eat into your long-term profits.

Some people can only start with $250 a month deposited into their account. If that is you, then I really applaud you. In this case, you would put all that money into a single stock so that you only have one trade commission to pay. Be sure to buy stock in a different company the next month and each following month. When you have built up a more balanced portfolio of at least 20 stocks, then you can start buying stock in a company that you already own, but only if the stock is a real bargain with a P/E of below 10.

BUILDING A WATCHLIST

It is impractical to search for and analyze more than 20 stocks a day by reading annual reports, recording prices, earnings figures and dividend figures. The only way to be able to analyze multiple stocks is to build a watch-list. There are many spreadsheet programs available, but I prefer to use Microsoft Excel, part of Office 365, which you can get from Microsoft for $6.99 a month. It is worth the investment.

My current watch-list, which I review annually, contains 940 stocks that are in the Mid Cap, Large Cap or Mega Cap and pay a dividend. I have set it up so that I can export the end of day stock prices from the TD Ameritrade platform that I use (Think or Swim) and import these prices directly into my watch-list spreadsheet. I have set it up so that the P/E is calculated automatically and all I have to do is sort the data based on the calculated P/E. I do this every trading day and make the results available to my subscribers on my website (www.briandeeker.com/subscribe).

Every day, there are usually at least 30 stocks available (often more than 40) with a P/E of less than 10. If I am setting up a new portfolio for a client, I will start with 40 and equally divide the initial investment amount by 40 to determine how much I am paying per company. If I am selling stock and buying stock in another company (more on this in chapter seven), then I will determine how much money is available and divide the money available by the number that is closest to making the amount the same as the other stocks in the portfolio.

For example, if I sold stock at a profit, I have the initial investment, plus the profit to spend on new stock. If I spent $2,500 on the initial stock purchase and have made $2,000 in profit (which is quite common), then I have $4,500 to spend on stock from companies not already in the portfolio. In this case, I would divide $4,500 by 2 = $2,250 and purchase stock in two new companies that are at the top of the watchlist when it has been sorted on the P/E.

To make sure that the portfolio stays balanced, try to buy stock in a company that you don't already own if the P/E is about the same as another stock that you currently have. However, if the P/E is below 5, then the stock is a real bargain and I will purchase more of the stock.

I go into more detail on the specifics of how to do the research and build the watch-list in chapter nine.

EXAMPLE PORTFOLIO

Today is November 30th, 2018 as I write this section. I tell you the date so that you can independently check these figures. The table below contains an example portfolio of the stocks that I would pick if I was doing this for a client right now. I have chosen stocks that are currently in the S&P 500.

The starting amount is $100,000 and the commission to be paid is $6.95 per company, no matter how many stocks are bought. I would have paid $98,492.37 buying the stocks and another $278.00 in commissions for a total spend of $98,770.37.

Symbol	Name	Buy Price	P/E	# Stocks	Spend
FCX	Freeport	$ 11.74	5.39	216	$2,535.84
NWL	Newell	$23.92	5.63	106	$2,535.52
PRU	Prudential	$93.47	5.72	27	$2,523.69
T	AT&T	$31.28	5.93	81	$2,533.28
KHC	Kraft	$51.00	5.99	50	$2,550.00
IP	Int. Paper	$46.23	6.04	55	$2,542.65
F	Ford	$9.42	6.07	266	$2,504.39
VIAB	Viacom	$30.81	6.20	82	$2,526.42
LYB	Lyondell	$92.85	6.20	28	$2,599.80
WRK	Westrock	$46.95	6.29	54	$2,535.30
M	Macys	$34.30	6.31	74	$2,538.20
TMK	Torchmark	$87.26	6.43	28	$2,412.74
PFG	Principal	$49.31	6.58	52	$2,564.12
KR	Kroger	$29.63	6.67	84	$2,488.92
LNC	Lincoln	$63.12	6.71	39	$2,436.88
PSX	Phillips 66	$92.07	6.93	26	$2,407.93
TSN	Tyson	$58.59	6.94	42	$2,441.41
AFL	Aflac	$45.73	7.17	54	$2,454.27
IVZ	Investco	$20.45	7.18	121	$2,479.55
HPE	Hewlett P E	$14.86	7.28	167	$2,485.15
EMN	Eastman	$79.05	7.33	31	$2,420.95
CMCSA	Comcast	$39.09	7.55	63	$2,460.91
VLO	Valero	$79.19	7.60	31	$2,420.81
VZ	Verizon	$59.89	7.62	41	$2,440.12
CNP	Centerpoint	$27.73	7.77	89	$2,472.27
AIV	Apartment	$46.45	7.97	53	$2,543.55
CTL	Centurylink	$18.73	7.97	132	$2,481.27
MPC	Marathon	$64.55	8.10	38	$2,435.45
SYF	Synchrony	$25.97	8.17	95	$2,474.03
HPQ	HP	$22.91	8.24	108	$2,477.09
NSC	Norfolk	$171.85	8.26	14	$2,328.15

Symbol	Name	Buy Price	P/E	# Stocks	Spend
STX	Seagate	$42.38	8.39	58	$2,457.62
AVGO	Broadcom	$236.02	8.48	10	$2,263.98
RE	Everest	$221.81	8.59	10	$2,278.19
LUV	Southwest	$53.98	8.61	45	$2,446.03
ALL	Allstate	$88.68	8.61	27	$2,411.32
TAP	Molson	$65.43	8.65	37	$2,434.57
AMG	Affiliated	$111.49	8.66	21	$2,388.51
SJM	Smucker	$103.78	8.77	23	$2,396.22
MET	Metlife	$44.72	8.84	55	$2,455.28

This portfolio would pay $3,447.39 in dividends for the first year with a dividend percentage of 3.45% (dividends don't change much, so the next few years would have a similar figure). This is better than any "safe" bonds available. The current yield for 10 Year US Treasury Bonds is 3.015% as of this writing and your money would be tied up for 10 years.

There is no way to know which stocks will do well in the short to medium term (1 – 5 years) because all these stocks are currently out of favor in the market. Some of them will rise very quickly, while others will drop even further in the short term. However, all of them are expected to rise in the long term and that is how you make your money.

CHAPTER SEVEN

When To Sell

No-one knows the optimal time to sell, but the P/E is a very good indicator. It is human nature to want a stock to keep rising forever and to hold on as long as possible. However, what is more likely is that the stock will reverse at some point and any profits you would have generated if you had sold are now lost. Emotions can run high and greed can take over. It is far better to take some profit, leaving some on the table than to lose those profits.

The two main reasons people lose money in the stock market is because of greed and fear. Both emotions have no place in the decision-making process of the professional investor. Greed will make an investor hold on to a stock far longer than they should and fear will cause an investor to sell a stock when they shouldn't. People that do this are speculators, not investors. The vast majority of people that buy stock are speculators, including most mutual and hedge fund managers.

Another major reason that people lose money in the stock market is that they get caught watching the charts. They think that the chart is going up and that they are safe letting the stock run some more, trying to squeeze every penny of profit out of the stock. They never look at the financial information on the company, which is the true indicator of when a stock price may fall. The stock may continue to run for a long time past a negative earnings report, or even a series of negative earnings because people follow the crowd.

Eventually, the market will catch up with a stock, realize that it is well over priced and the stock will fall as investors dump the stock by the millions. When that happens, the stock price will plummet, and your gains can be wiped out in hours.

SELLING WHEN THE P/E IS POSITIVE

I always hold on to a stock for at least a year for the tax advantages (more on that in chapter eight) and then use the P/E to determine if the stock needs to be sold. I check the portfolio every year and if the P/E is over 40 and the stock is in profit, I sell the stock.

When a stock is doing well, showing consistent positive earnings and the stock price is rising, I check the stock every year. Otherwise, I leave it alone. This allows a stock to run, but also ensures that the stock is still reasonably priced by the market. I check the stock every year and if the P/E is over 40, I sell it and buy stock in companies that have a much better P/E of under 10, using the initial money I paid for the stock and the profits generated by the sale. If the P/E is under 40, the market has priced the stock fairly well, and it probably has more profit available.

You will see ridiculous P/E levels of well over 100 for some stock, but the market simply has not caught up with the discrepancy yet. It is only a matter of time before the stock price returns to a more realistic level. Stocks will reach these high P/E ratios when they are in favor and everyone is buying them.

Amazon is a good example of this with a P/E of 96.15 and a stock price of $1,713.10 at the time of this writing. However, stocks like this usually crash when they are most popular, and millions of people will often lose money on the stock. I prefer to make my profit early and sell when the P/E is above 40, which is usually when everyone else starts to buy.

This approach forces you to rebalance your portfolio, effectively making you take the profits when they are there and buying stock in other companies. This reduces your risk significantly and ensures that you don't have any stock that is ready for a major move downward. If you let a stock run for anything longer than a year when the P/E is over 40, your risk of losing the profits increases and your portfolio is out of balance.

The risk to reward ratio becomes too high and your chance of selling at a loss increase significantly since your mindset will become negatively affected. Eventually stock prices will fall, and your emotions will fall with it, probably leading to a bad decision to sell at a loss and look for something better.

Rebalancing your portfolio like this will protect you from

yourself and ensure that you are successful for many years to come. You want to be a successful investor with a long-term approach, rather than a speculator who is out of the market in a year or less.

SELLING WHEN THE P/E IS NEGATVE

I also sell a stock when there are negative earnings reported for the company for the last 12 months (Trailing Twelve Months or TTM). However, don't sell the stock if it is not in profit, simply hold on to it until the company recovers.

Remember the recent energy crisis when Saudi Arabia flooded the market with their oil as cheaply as they could in 2014? There were some other contributing factors as well, such as the slowing of the Chinese economy, but the actions by Saudi Arabia were certainly the main contributing factor. This wiped out a lot of the smaller players in the oil industry and companies such as Cimarex Energy (XEC) and NRG Energy (NRG), both in the S&P 500, reported negative earnings.

I didn't have XEC or NRG in my portfolio at the time, but I would have sold them immediately if the stock had already been in profit, even if that profit was only a dollar. XEC has since recovered, but NRG is still reporting negative earnings even now. If you can sell a stock when the earnings are negative, but you have already made a profit, then sell it. You don't want to own stock in a company that may be on a downward spiral.

Very few things will demoralize you more that holding on to a stock in the hope that it will rise again. If you can get rid of an under achieving stock when it has already made you profit, you are going to be a much more confident investor. Follow these principles and you will maintain a strong investor mindset that allows you to buy stocks when no-one else can see the potential and sell them when everyone else wants to buy.

CHAPTER EIGHT

Tax Implications

Nothing will eat into your profits more than the tax man. Your job as an investor is to legally minimize your taxes as much as possible so that you can re-invest that money and take advantage of the power of compound interest. There is nothing patriotic about paying too much in taxes. In fact, it is your right as a citizen of the United States (or any other country) to minimize your taxes as much as is legally allowed.

Every profit you make is taxed at some level. If you are making regular trades as a short-term trader, all profitable trades are taxed at your current tax bracket. Even if your losses are taken into consideration (remember rule number one – never lose money), you still pay tax on the profits for the year. So, for every $100 gain you make, you can lose up to $37 of your profits, depending on your income level recorded with the IRS, which will significantly reduce your overall investment return.

If you made $100,000 in trading profit for the last year on a $1 million portfolio, your return is 10%. Not bad, you think to yourself. But how much are you really keeping? Assuming that you sold the stock after holding it for less than a year, which is a typical trading scenario, and you earn $120,000 in wages, then your return is actually 7.69% and you would be required to pay $23,100 in taxes according to the current tax rates published by the IRS at the time of this writing. Ouch!

What if you made the same $100,000 in profit on the same $1 million portfolio, but had kept the stock for over a year? Your results are vastly different. Assuming the same $120,000 annual salary, you would only be required to pay $15,000 in taxes and your return would jump up to 8.5%. That's $8,100 in your pocket that you can re-invest.

If you were able to duplicate these conditions for the next 10 years, you have an additional $81,000 to invest. It all adds up. Of course, these results are hypothetical, but you get the concept.

The maximum tax bracket at the time of this writing is 37%. The threshold is different for single or married filing jointly, but the effect is the same. Every dollar you earn over $500,000 for a single person, or $600,000 for a married couple is taxed at 37% and that tax rate will apply to all your profit if you sold the stock within a year. If you waited for a year or more, then the maximum you can pay is 20% and most people will only pay 15% on the profits.

If you have invested in a mutual or hedge fund, then you are always taxed at the highest level possible because they constantly buy and sell stock within a year. To make matters worse, all you have to do is be a part of the mutual fund, even if you bought into it at close to the end of the year, and you will be required to pay taxes on the whole profit for the year, even if you didn't actually receive the profit.

Tax will ruin your retirement unless it is managed correctly. Always let your investments sit for at least 365 days before you ever consider selling them.

CHAPTER NINE

How To Get The Data You Need

Building a watch-list containing the best companies to invest in and data collection are the two most important parts of the investment process because the watch-list enables you to make good investment decisions on what to buy and sell. If your earnings figures are out, or you have the wrong stock price, then your calculations are flawed, and the stock may not be as good as you think it is. It is also nice to have the correct dividend amount, although this is not as crucial as having the correct earnings figures to be able to calculate the correct Price to Earnings ratio (P/E).

If you get stuck with anything in this chapter, I have prepared a daily watch-list spreadsheet and video series which you can access on my site at www.briandeeker.com/subscribe. The daily watch-list and video series are part of a subscription service I provide. You can have access to my daily watch-list, which contains all the calculations I use to build and manage the portfolios of my clients along with unlimited access to all the videos, which will teach you everything you need to know.

Check it out at www.briandeeker.com/subscribe.

This chapter is the most technical of the book. It relies on your having a basic knowledge of Microsoft Excel. If you are unfamiliar with Excel, I suggest you learn Excel for free by doing a Google search "learn Excel for free". There are a lot of good free tutorials that will teach you all the basics you need to be able to follow along.

HOW TO BUILD A WATCH LIST

The watch-list is your go-to resource for data collection and manipulation and will allow you to make quick and accurate decisions based on the financial data that you collect. If you don't have a watch-list with reliable data, you can't make good investment decisions and you will probably lose your investment capital.

You can get the list of Mid Cap, Large Cap and Mega Cap companies from the following URL on the NASDAQ site:

https://www.nasdaq.com/screening/companies-by-industry.aspx

Look to the menu on the left and scroll down to see the links. The spreadsheet manipulation is similar for the S&P 500, which is what I will be focusing on during this chapter.

The list of companies in the S&P 500 is surprisingly difficult to get, considering how often it is referenced in the financial world. You can get it for a hefty price from Standard & Poor's own website by contacting their sales department. However, there is a better way. Go to the SPDR® S&P 500® ETF (SPY) website at https://us.spdrs.com/en/etf/spdr-sp-500-etf-SPY and click on the Holdings tab. Look for a link at the bottom of the table and click "Download All Holdings". This will download an excel spreadsheet with all the information you need.

You now have a lot of data in the spreadsheet, but you don't need all of it. Delete the top 3 rows. You want the Name and Identifier columns, so highlight all the other columns and press "Delete" on your keyboard. You should now have 2 columns of data. Change the "Identifier" heading to "Symbol", make it the first column and bold the headings (Figure 1):

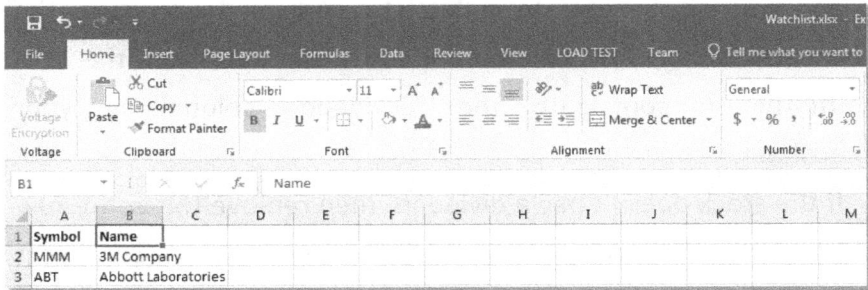

Figure 1.

Save your file as an Excel file to your computer where you can find it again with the name "Watchlist" (Watchlist.xlsx). This is the start of your watch-list, where you will include dividend and earnings data. If you scroll down, you will see that the S&P 500 has 505 companies in the list at the time of this writing.

The next step is to add a heading next to "Name" called "Dividend" (Figure 2):

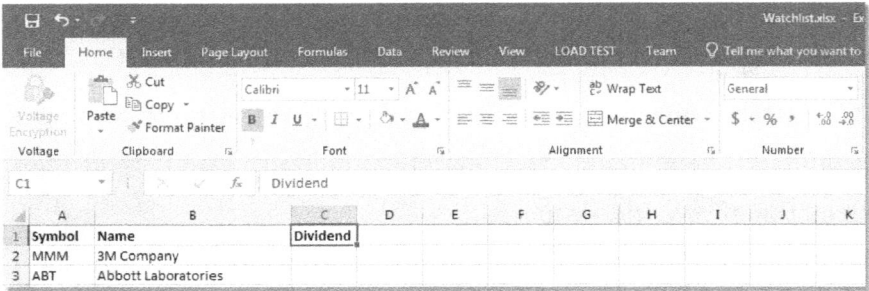

Figure 2.

The dividend determines if the stock makes the watch-list and if a company doesn't pay a dividend, remove it from the list. You can get the dividend data for free from morningstar.com. Simply copy the symbol and paste it into the search bar, click on the "Dividends" tab and you will be able to collect the current dividend for the stock. Look for the TTM column and enter the data from the TTM on morningstar.com into the "Dividend" column in your spreadsheet.

If the stock doesn't pay a dividend, then remove the entire row by highlighting the row and then right clicking on the row and select "Delete". If the stock does pay a dividend, paste it into the spreadsheet in the Dividend column next to the Name column (Figure 3):

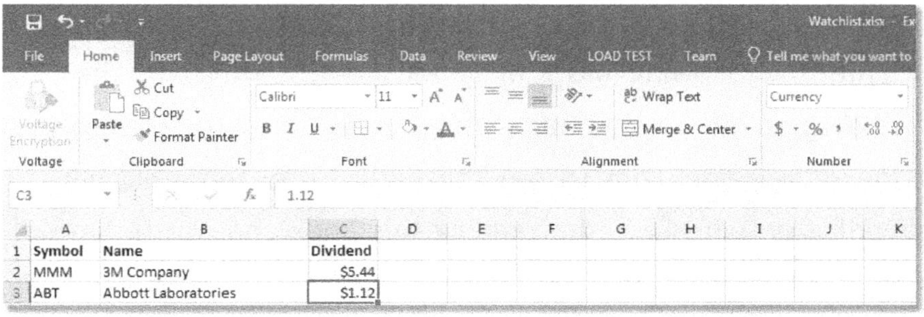

Figure 3.

HOW TO COLLECT EARNINGS DATA

Earnings data is the most important data you can collect since it is a financial snapshot of how the company is performing right now. If the earnings figures are negative or low, then the company is performing poorly, no matter what their marketing team and CEO may say. If the earnings figures are consistently strong, then the company is in a strong financial position and the stock is worth buying if the P/E is below 10.

There are many online resources that are reliable and have the earnings data you need. Most of them are a paid service, but the one I use is free and is run by Morningstar. Another good place to find free earnings data is the NASDAQ website. For the purposes of teaching in this book, I will use Morningstar.

Enter the stock symbol in the search bar on morningstar.com and click on the "Financials" tab. The earnings data is the row called "Diluted Earnings Per Share" and shows the last 5 years for a free account and the last 10 years for the paid subscription. You will need the earnings figures for the last 5 years, so stick with the free version.

Enter the following into your spreadsheet, starting with the first year (2013 at the time of this writing). Move the scroll bar to the left on morningstar.com to see the data. Note, this will change, depending on when you are reading this book and at the time of writing (December 2018), the figures for 2013 are still showing on morningstar.com. The figure you are looking for is the "Diluted Earnings Per Share". Enter the data into your spreadsheet for all stocks and years as follows (Figure 4):

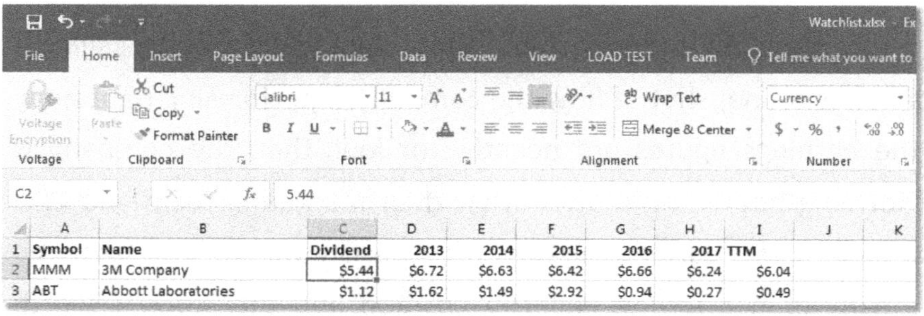

Figure 4.

If you look at Figure 4, the earnings for both companies are positive, but there is a difference. The earnings for MMM are consistently strong and positive, but the earnings for ABT are still positive, but have dropped recently. If earnings suddenly drop like this, then there may be financial problems for the company in the future and you would avoid buying stock in this company until the earnings return to previous levels. The P/E ratio will give you the best indication as to when to buy (see chapter five).

Collect the data for all companies for the last 5 years, including the Trailing Twelve Months (TTM) and format the cells to show negative earnings in red. This will help you see which companies are strong financially and which are not.

COLLECTING THE END OF DAY (EOD) STOCK PRICES

When you collect the End of Day (EOD) stock prices depends entirely on what is happening in your trading account. If you are making regular monthly payments, you would collect the EOD stock prices each month. If you have made a single payment to your account (e.g. $100,000) and are not making any more payments, then you would collect the EOD stock prices every year.

The worst thing you can do is to look at the stock prices each day because you will start becoming obsessed about your account balance. Your stocks need room to mature and they can certainly drop below what you paid for them. If you are monitoring the prices each day, you will eventually crack and end up selling them at precisely the wrong time for less than what you paid for them. Let your stocks mature for at least a year before you check them again so that you keep your sanity and account balance intact.

When it is time to check the stock prices, you can do it one of two ways. You can either Google the stock price and manually enter it into your spreadsheet, or you can export the data from somewhere else and import it into your spreadsheet. The second approach is the one I prefer and is the one I teach in this book.

I use TD Ameritrade's Think or Swim platform to place all my trades because I can also export the EOD stock price data with the platform. Contact TD Ameritrade directly to set up Think or Swim and to learn how to export the EOD data (I also do a video of this on my site at www.briandeeker.com/subscribe). Export your EOD data after 3pm Eastern so that you can be ready to buy or sell your stocks the next day. The export will be in CSV format and will have the current stock price for each symbol. The EOD stock prices will enable you to determine the P/E for each stock in your watch-list, which will show you when it is time to buy and sell.

IMPORTING THE DATA

Importing the data into your spreadsheet is quite simple. Open the CSV sheet in Excel by clicking File → Open →The name of the CSV file. By default, Excel is looking for an xlsx file and the CSV file will not show. Change the selector dropdown to "All Files" and you will be able to select the CSV file. Click "Open", select "Delimited" → Next → Comma → Next → "General" → Finish (Figure 5).

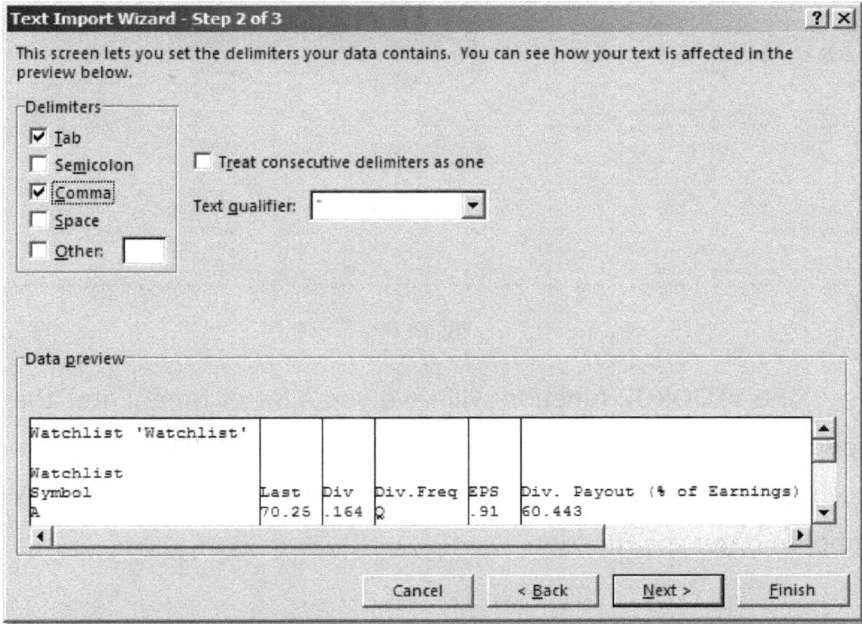

Figure 5.

Copy the sheet by hitting CTRL + A and then CTRL + C and then paste the values into a new sheet on your watch-list. Call the new sheet "Data". This will allow you to search the data for the current price for each stock by using the VLOOKUP function. If you get stuck with the VLOOKUP function, do a Google search for it. There are plenty of easy to follow tutorials available. There is a video on this on my site at www.briandeeker.com/subscribe.

Your first sheet contains all the data you have been collecting from Morningstar. Rename the sheet "Essential Data" or something similar. Add another heading next to TTM called "Current Price". It should look like this (Figure 6):

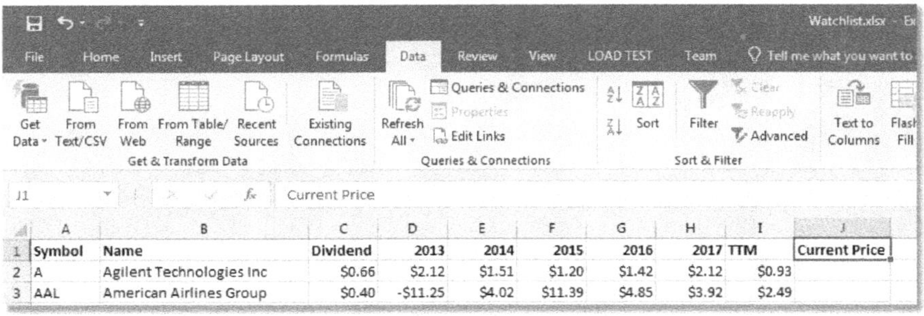

Figure 6.

The VLOOKUP function will save you a lot of time. Enter the following into the cell below "Current Price": =vlook (Figure 7). The Excel prompt will come up and you double click on the small *fx* symbol to enter the function.

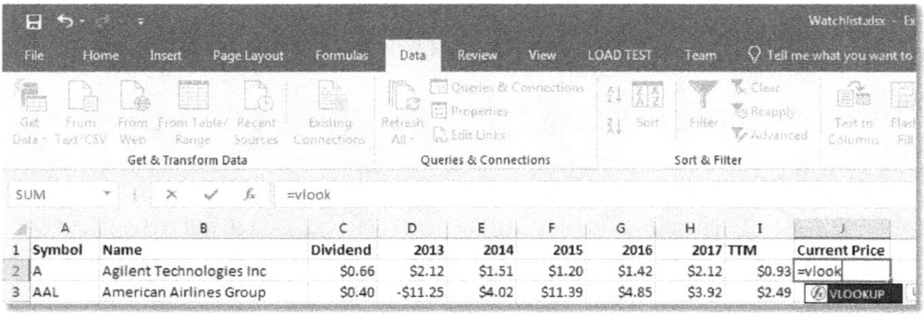

Figure 7.

You then click on the other *fx* symbol (next to the check mark or tick) highlighted as follows (Figure 8):

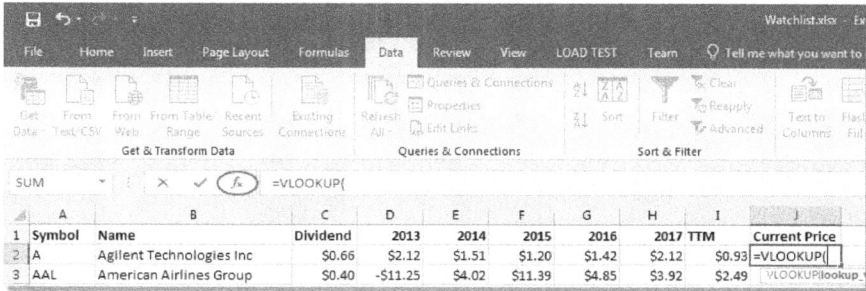

Figure 8.

This will take you into the Excel dialog box that will allow you to search for the stock price based on the stock symbol (Figure 9).

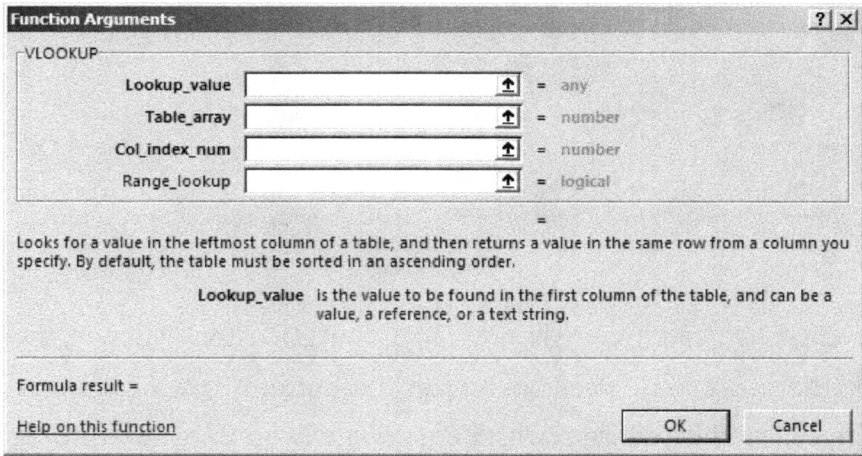

Figure 9.

You are automatically taken to the first field called Lookup_value. Select the first symbol in the list under the "Symbol" heading (cell A1, Figure 8). Press the tab key on the keyboard. You are now in the Table_array field. Click on the sheet at the bottom of the spreadsheet called "Data". You are now taken to the Col_index_num field. Select both columns in the "Data" sheet and press tab on the keyboard. Enter "2" into the Col_index_num field since you want the data in the second column. Finally, hit tab on the keyboard and type "false" in the Range_lookup field. This will return an exact value. If you have done it right, it should look like this (Figure 10):

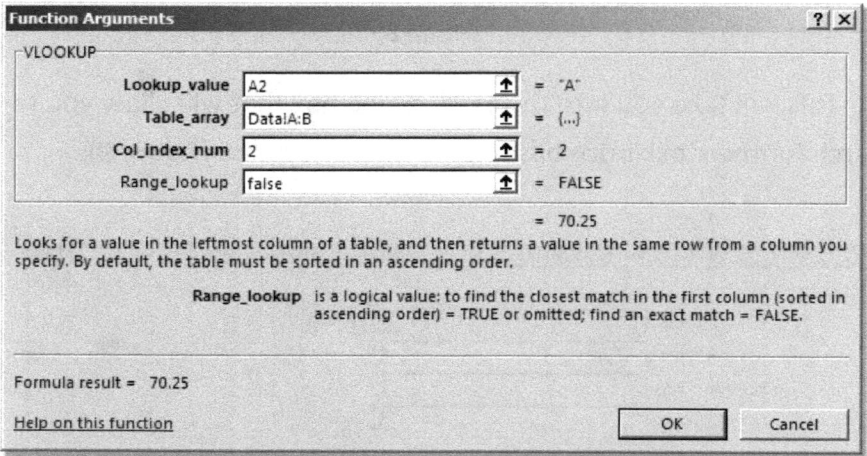

Figure 10.

Click "OK" and you will now have the EOD stock price in the cell. There is a very small square on the bottom right of the cell. Double click this square and the equation will be transferred to all cells below it until it gets to the end of the data. You now have the current EOD stock prices for all the stocks in your watch-list, which saves you many hours of data entry and ensures accuracy.

The best thing about the VLOOKUP function is that the function remains in the cell and it will always look for the data in the "Data" tab for the corresponding symbol. If you paste new values in the "Data" tab, either in a month or a year, by following the data export and import process mentioned previously, the formula will display the new stock price for you.

Don't worry, if you are getting stuck, I provide a full video series at www.briandeeker.com/subscribe.

CALCULATE THE P/E

You now have all the data you need to calculate the P/E, showing you when to buy and when to sell. The P/E is simply the current price divided by the TTM (Trailing Twelve Months) earnings figure.

Go back to the "Essential Data" sheet and create a new heading called P/E as follows (Figure 11):

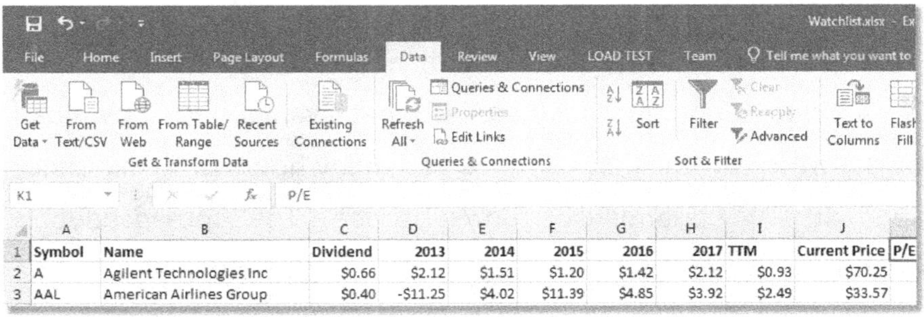

Figure 11.

Move to the cell below the P/E heading and type the following: =J2/I2 and press enter. This will give you the P/E for that stock. Double click the small square icon at the bottom right of the cell to copy the function to all the data cells. Right click the column and select "Format cells". Select "Number" and then choose formatting to two decimal places to make the numbers easier to read.

I also like to highlight any cells that are negative by going to the

"Home" tab, clicking "Conditional Formatting" → "Highlight Cell Rules" → "Less Than" → 0 → select "Red Text" and click "OK". This will draw my eye to any negative values. Remember, you don't want to buy a stock with a negative P/E.

You now have the P/E for each of the stocks, but you will have to sort them. Click the "Data" tab and select everything by hitting CTRL + A. Click sort and then sort by P/E in the dropdown selector. The sort function is at the top of the spreadsheet in a tab also called "Data". This is different from the "Data" tab that you created. This will sort the values smallest to largest. All the negative P/E values will be at the top and the real bargains will be the values that are positive and below 10. Any stock with a P/E of between 15 and 40 is reasonably priced by the market and anything over 40 is overpriced and is at risk of a price drop.

If you are having problems with any of these calculations, I have a video series and daily spreadsheet available for download that is always current that will save you many hours of work. Check it out at www.briandeeker.com/subscribe. The spreadsheet is available for download each day and is always current with the latest stock prices, earnings and dividend data and has all the calculations done for you. The video series is available as part of the subscription and covers everything you need to know.

CHAPTER TEN

Why Other Investments Don't Work

There are so many investment choices available, most of which will trap the unwary, and by their very nature will cause you to lose money. In case you are tempted to try any of these, I thought it best to let you know what you are getting into and your chances of succeeding with them. Let's start with Bonds, the most common of all.

BONDS

Everybody loves bonds. You can buy them from most large companies, the US government, states, counties and even foreign companies and governments. But what is a bond? A bond is a promise to repay a debt, nothing more. The issuer promises to repay the money at a fixed interest rate over a specific time period ranging from 3 months to 100 years.

Most people believe that bonds are safe, are highly suited to a long-term investment approach and are immune to market crashes. Most investment professionals will even recommend a higher percentage of bonds when people get closer to retirement. But how safe are they really? Well, the answer is that it depends on the issuer. Most bonds lost value during the stock market crash of 2008 and a lot of people lost money. Even the yields of long-term US Treasury bonds dropped sharply.

It is commonly assumed that bonds are unaffected by stock market crashes and they continue to pay the same, no matter what happens. However, this assumption is not only wrong, it is dangerous. During the market crash of 2008, there was a 0.8 correlation with stocks, meaning that bonds and stocks dropped at almost the same rate.

Bonds have a rating system controlled by Moody's, Fitch and Standard & Poor's, that rates the risk of the issuer. It is a lot like an individual's credit report except it refers to the company or government agency. The higher the rating, the lower the risk. However, there is still risk and the chances of losing all your money in bonds does exist. If a company files for Chapter 11 bankruptcy, there is a chance that you will lose all your money that you have tied up in their bonds. The only truly risk-free bonds are US Treasury bonds and the returns on these are pitiful. Currently, 30-year TIPS have a return of 1.235% according to Reuters.

To get a higher return than this, you would have to consider a lower bond rating and the risk increases with the return. There is even a grade called "Junk Bonds" that pay a higher return. They are called junk for a reason because there is a significant risk that you may lose all your money. Currently, the average yield of junk bonds is 6.02%, down 40% from 10% in 2016. Do you really want to tie up your money for 10 years or more with the risk that you may lose all of it?

I often get a better than 6% annual return on the dividends alone on some of the stocks in my portfolio. There is only a very minimal risk of the companies going bankrupt because the stocks I invest in are in the Mid Cap, Large Cap, Mega Cap or S&P 500.

Stay away from bonds. They should come with a bright red warning label.

DAY TRADING AND FOREX TRADING USING TECHNICAL ANALYSIS

Technical Analysis is used by most day traders and FOREX traders. It is a system of chart recognition patters that attempt to predict what is going to happen to the stock or FOREX price based on what has happened previously. Some of the chart patterns actually do work a lot of the time, but not all the time. It is so easy to base a trade off a pattern only to be completely wrong.

To counter the possibility of being wrong, traders will set a stop loss to minimize their losses as much as possible. However, a lot of the time, the stop loss will be triggered due to a minor market reversal and then continue in the direction that the trader anticipated. The result being that they were right and still lost money.

Stop losses will slowly eat away at your account balance and will cause you to lose sleep. They sound like they are a good idea in theory. However, they are the reason most traders lose money. A few small losses here, a small loss there quickly add up and before you know it, you have lost half of your investment capital. Once you have lost half of your initial investment money, you will start to take risks to make the money back, causing even further losses. To break even after losing half of your account balance, you need to make a 100% return on your money, which could take years. In fact, it will probably never happen.

Day trading also encourages chart watching, which will eat up all your time, energy and sanity in the long term. Chart watching can be quite mesmerizing and will eventually take over from everything else, at the expense of your family, friends and other interests. You will get to the point of being scared to leave your seat in case you miss the next major move. I started as a trader and as a result, I nearly walked away from investing because of the losses I took.

MUTUAL FUNDS

Mutual funds are the ultimate money-making machine for the fund managers. Their returns are awful, and their fees are high. See chapter three for the fees charged by mutual funds. These fees are so well hidden, you need a magnifying glass to read the fine print.

The mutual fund companies will start 5 mutual funds in the hope that they all will take off, knowing that probably only one will do well. Quite often, none of them do well. When a fund does post a return better than the S&P 500 Index, usually by luck, they will start advertising their "amazing" returns to attract more investors. Investors flood in looking for the same high returns, but usually the funds return to their mediocre returns. 96% of mutual fund managers are not able to beat the S&P 500 Index. Those that do are rarely the same funds each year.

Think of it this way. You can train a gorilla to flip a coin ten times in a row. If you put 1,024 gorillas in a warehouse and have them all flip a coin ten times, one of them will flip heads ten times in a row. Most people would call that luck, but the investment companies will call him a genius and put him in charge of their next fund. What are the chances that the same gorilla will flip heads ten times in a row again?

HEDGE FUNDS

Hedge funds returns are as bad as mutual funds and most hedge fund managers cannot beat the S&P 500 Index. Hedge funds are very lucrative for the fund owners and managers, but their fees are also very high. A typical hedge fund will charge 2% of the initial investment and 20% of the profits.

There is a lot less scrutiny of hedge funds than mutual funds because hedge funds are generally only available to accredited investors. The Securities and Exchange Commission (SEC) takes the view that accredited investors can afford to lose their money, so most hedge funds are left alone.

Hedge funds make their money in fees, even when they have a

losing year. You will be charged no matter what their return is. You put up all the money, take all the risk and only get to keep some of the profits when the fund does well and will still be charged when the fund loses money.

Some hedge funds, such as the funds offered by Bridgewater Associates do consistently beat the S&P 500. However, Bridgewater is not taking on new investors.

GOLD

Gold is often touted as the only safe investment there is with a guaranteed return. However, there is no guaranteed return with gold. It does not pay a dividend or any interest. It costs you money to store it and there is no guarantee that gold prices will increase. From 1988 to 2005, the price of gold remained between $256 and $500 per ounce and was flatlining. In 2012, the price of gold peaked at $1,864 and has dropped since then to $1,246 at the time of this writing.

Investors will flock to gold in times of financial crisis in the hope that gold will prove to be a more stable investment, but the data does not back that up. Gold is a commodity and gold prices are governed by demand. As fear increases, more people buy gold and the price goes up in the short term. However, gold is not a good investment in the long term.

OPTIONS AND FUTURES

An option is a purchased contract that gives the buyer the right to buy or sell a stock at a pre-determined price. Options do not come cheap and are usually around 5 - 20% of the purchase price of the stock, depending on the time available in the option. Each option has a length of time attached to it for the buyer to be able to exercise his right to purchase the stock at the agreed price. Loosely translated, if you buy an option, you usually have only a few months to a year for the stock price to move enough to be attractive enough to buy or sell the stock at the option price (termed "call" or "put").

If the option is close to the stock price (termed "in the money"), then the price of the option is more than if it is a long way from the current price (termed "out of the money"). For example, you could buy an option for very little money if the option price is $10 above the current stock price for a call and $10 below the current price for a put. However, the chances of collecting are slim because the price of the stock must move $10 plus the amount you paid for the option for you to make any money on it. Also, the more time available on the option, the more expensive it is.

Most options expire worthless and the money is lost. You can be right in your analysis that the stock will move in a certain direction and still lose money if the market does not move fast enough. Options are based solely on statistical analysis of price movement.

Futures are like options in that you can lock in an agreed price for a commodity over a set period of time. This is good for farmers and businesses that rely on set pricing (such as McDonalds locking in the price of beef for a year) so that they can plan for the long term. However, there is a price to be paid for futures and they are not cheap.

There is no guarantee that prices will increase in the long term and you can be left with a futures contract that is worthless if the actual price at the end of the contract is less than the price on the purchased contract.

REAL ESTATE

Real Estate investing is a lot riskier than people think. It can work but is not worth the risk in my opinion. It hit its height just prior to the stock market crash of 2008 and was fueled by bad lending practices. Prior to the crash, it seemed that all you needed was a pulse to qualify for a loan and invest in a real estate deal. People were borrowing far more than they could repay to invest in real estate. Consequently, many people lost everything they had, including their homes.

Even today, people will invest in a second home as a rental property and pay more in mortgage repayments than they are paid in rent in the hope that the price of the home will increase in the future and they can sell the house at a profit. This is called negative gearing. If you can sell at a profit (by no means guaranteed) there are still taxes to pay on the capital gain. Unless the money is rolled over into another investment property, you will pay tax at your current tax bracket on all the profit generated. You will also have to pay closing costs and agent commissions.

Let's look at a typical deal: a 3-bedroom, 2-bathroom house in the suburbs of many American cities. If the purchase price is $100,000, your typical rental income is around $800 - $1,000 a month, depending on location. At best, your return is 12% for the year, but will most probably be a lot less. Vacancy rates are usually around 5 - 10% and you are responsible for any repairs.

Ask any landlord and they will tell you how much it costs to maintain a house. If it cost you $4,000 in maintenance and repairs for the year and you had the house vacant for a month, then your return is only 7% at best. All the operating expenses come out of your pocket, reducing your annual return. Don't forget taxes and insurance, those must be paid too.

If you want real estate deals to work financially, be prepared to buy a house that needs a lot of work. You also run the risk of buying someone else's problem and sinking a lot more money into the deal than you budgeted for to make it work. Real estate investing can work, but there is considerable risk.

PEER TO PEER LENDING AND EQUITY CROWDFUNDING

Peer to peer lending is quite new and involves multiple people financing business and personal loans. In my opinion, there is nothing riskier than peer to peer lending because there is no way to guarantee that the loan will be repaid. There is no collateral, no guarantee that the business will succeed and no way to collect if everything goes bad. If you do take the business or person to court in the event of non-payment, your chances of recovering all your money are minimal at best.

Equity crowdfunding involves buying shares in startup companies that have no history of positive earnings and nothing to offer other than an idea and a dream. Most startups fail miserably and the probability of losing all your money is around 95%. Equity crowdfunding is a home run swing with nothing to fall back on if the company fails.

BANK PRODUCTS

A CD is a Certificate of Deposit, usually offered by banks and credit unions. You enter into a contract with the financial institution for them to hold your money for a certain length of time, usually 6 months to 5 years, in exchange for a guaranteed rate of return. They are like a savings account, but there is no way to withdraw your money without paying hefty fees.

Back in the 1980s, you could invest in a CD and get paid up to 14% return on your money, but those days are long gone. Only a few years ago, they were paying 0.15% and as of this writing are hovering around 3%. That barely covers the current inflation rate of 1.9%, effectively giving you a 1% return on your money.

The CD is only as strong as the issuing bank and if the bank goes out of business, your money is difficult to get back. According to the Federal Deposit Insurance Corporation (FDIC), there have been 555 bank failures since 2000. The owners of the CDs are insured to at least $250,000, but for amounts exceeding that, the money is lost with no recourse for the buyer.

CHAPTER ELEVEN

The Responsibility of Wealth

I wanted to include a chapter on the responsibility of wealth because it is not often talked about in the financial world. Does wealth bring responsibility? I think it does. It is easy to be selfish and hoard your wealth for yourself, but in the end, you are only serving yourself and not the greater good.

I was fortunate enough to be born in Australia, later moving to the US to become a citizen. But not everyone is so fortunate. If you live in the western world and have a job, you are already wealthier than more than half of the world's population. A lot of the people in poorer nations struggle to find regular food and water and most don't have the modern conveniences of cars, air conditioning and heating that we take for granted.

I think with wealth comes great responsibility to help those that can't help themselves. There is a direct correlation with the wealth level you get to and the amount you regularly give to others. Whether you call it the way of universe, karma or God, there is something that we can't control, or even understand, that directs our financial path and prosperity level. Start to tune into that and your wealth will increase. If you are regularly giving to others, it will come back to you.

Be generous. It is fun and brings great joy into your life. If you don't know what cause to give to, maybe you could start with your family.

There are many terrific causes run by kind and generous people that would love it if you would reach out to them. If your passion is to help people, look for ways to do that by providing better living conditions such as running water, digging wells, better food or better accommodations. If your passion is for the environment or animal welfare, there are many great organizations to donate to.

A great rule to live by is to give away 10% of everything you earn (before tax). Try it and you will see it return to you. I know that this is counter-intuitive, but I have seen it work in my own life. I started doing this over 15 years ago and I can look back in my life and see when the prosperity started to flow. It is when I started giving.

It really doesn't matter who, or what you give your money to, so long as you start giving. Starting small will train your mind to start thinking differently, from a mindset that focuses on what you don't have to a mindset where anything is possible. There is no greater joy than knowing that you have directly affected someone else's life for the better, knowing that you were able to make a difference.

As you become wealthier, you can give much more and still have everything you could possibly want in life. That is where true contentment and peace comes from, knowing that you are making a difference in other people's lives.

Living is giving. If you are not giving, you are not truly living.

CHAPTER TWELVE

About The Author

I am a professional investor and fund manager (accredited investors and foreign investors only), with over 20 years' experience investing in the US and foreign stock markets. I have no formal university qualifications (which is exactly the way I like it) and everything I teach has been learned through experience. If I had gone to Harvard like most fund managers, you would not be taught anything new and this investment approach would not exist.

I developed my investment approach prior to taking on clients to protect myself from the many stock losses I was suffering by following the advice of others. I realized that for every 10% loss, I had to make an 11% gain just to break even and I needed a way to invest without risk. This book is a result of that journey.

If you are interested in my fund management services, please go to www.briandeeker.com/fund-management. My fee is 0.5% of the investment amount under management.

APPENDIX

My Trades from January 2010 to January 2019

I started with $150,000 and invested in 40 stocks on January 19th, 2010, most with a P/E of below 10 and the highest P/E of 11.67.

The account balance as of February 1st, 2019 is $437,749.94 and the average annual return during this time is 13.54%, compared with a 9.91% average annual return for the S&P 500 during the same period. Had I bought stock in the SPDR® S&P 500® ETF (SPY) during the same period, I would have approximately $330,000.00 in my account (estimate based on the returns recorded of the SPY).

I have summarized my results, including the stocks that I sold and subsequently bought, in the following pages:

Total amount invested:	**$149,989.50**
Commissions paid:	**$278**

SUMMARY

Stocks Still in Portfolio

Symbol	Name	Shares	Buy Price
CIM	Chimera Investment	182	$4.13
MFA	MFA Financial	519	$7.23
WH	Wyndham Hotels & Resorts	1,157	$3.24
AFG	American Financial Group	148	$25.38
NNI	Nelnet	220	$17.05
CB	Chubb Limited	75	$50.02
RE	Everest Re Group	44	$85.36
TMK	Torchmark Corporation	180	$46.68
TRV	The Travelers Companies	77	$48.93
LMT	Lockheed Martin Corporation	48	$77.49
PKG	Packaging Corporation	158	$23.75
UNM	Unum Group	174	$21.53
UGI	UGI Corporation	230	$24.53
WFC	Wells Fargo	134	$28.05
HI	Hillenbrand	205	$18.28
TU	TELUS Corporation	236	$31.85
ECA	Encana Corporation	108	$34.63
EXC	Exelon Corporation	77	$48.73
RTN	Raytheon Company	69	$54.40
APU	AmeriGas Partners	90	$41.70
UNH	UnitedHealth Group	105	$35.37

Symbol	Name	Shares	Buy Price
AGO	Assured Guaranty	210	$19.06
AVY	Avery Dennison Corporation	96	$41.79
ALE	Allete, Inc.	83	$43.85
F	Ford Motor Company	259	$14.02
CLF	Cleveland-Cliffs	98	$37.12
HFC	HollyFrontier Corporation	82	$44.17
BXMT	Capital Trust	138	$28.05
TWO	Two Harbors Investments	198	$9.82
NLY	Annaly Capital Management	374	$10.35
PHM	PulteGroup	200	$19.33
MA	Mastercard Incorporated	47	$82.02
HPQ	HP Inc.	389	$9.74
TRN	Trinity Industries	189	$20.07
NVO	Novo Nordisk	69	$55.12
DAN	Dana Incorporated	334	$11.34
TGNA	TEGNA	161	$23.50
BNS	Bank of Nova Scotia	101	$37.57
MPC	Marathon Petroleum	89	$42.60
LYG	Lloyds Banking Group	1,098	$3.34
RIG	Transocean	239	$15.33
AGO	Assured Guaranty	91	$40.10
BAX	Baxter International	80	$46.04
LFC	China Life Insurance Company	266	$13.74
CIM	Chimera Investment	207	$17.70
CM	Canadian Imperial Bank	43	$85.80
DAL	Delta Air Lines	73	$50.27

Symbol	Name	Shares	Buy Price
PK	Park Hotels & Resorts	131	$29.72
ERF	Enerplus Corporation	338	$11.55
CVE	Cenovus Energy	366	$10.67
NLY	Annaly Capital Management	354	$11.03
NGG	National Grid Transco	68	$57.17
DRE	Duke Realty Corporation	150	$25.95
PTR	PetroChina Company	48	$80.99
EXG	Eaton Vance Income Fund	400	$9.75
TECK	Teck Resources	133	$29.40
LFC	China Life Insurance Company	264	$12.32
BTI	British American Tobacco	91	$35.67
CNX	CNX Resources Corporation	282	$11.52
R	Ryder System	55	$58.88
PRU	Prudential Financial	35	$92.52

Note: My stock portfolio grew from 40 stock positions in 2010 to 62 stocks positions in 2019, each of which is still paying me a dividend. My income from dividends went from $6,362.35 in 2010 to $13,425.09 in 2019.

Stocks Sold

Symbol	Name	Buy Price	Sell Price	Profit
HUN	Huntsman Corp.	$12.42	$17.58	$1,558.32
CF	CF Industries	$97.98	$144.52	$1,768.52
AEE	Ameren Corp.	$27.42	$28.41	$135.63
MAC	Macerich	$33.45	$47.61	$1,585.92
RNR	RenaissanceRe	$54.48	$72.93	$1,273.05
ADC	Agree Realty	$23.31	$25.38	$333.27
BIP	Brookfield	$17.00	$36.85	$4,386.85
WY	Weyerhaeuser	$21.51	$30.89	$1,744.68
TRGP	Targa Resources	$41.97	$59.27	$1,245.60
ITT	ITT Inc.	$22.01	$25.47	$477.48
MFC	Manulife	$11.92	$14.58	$678.30
DFS	Discover	$14.73	$53.39	$9,858.30
GD	General Dynamics	$70.40	$95.94	$1,353.62
BG	Bunge Limited	$71.70	$81.13	$527.80
AIZ	Assurant	$30.52	$78.89	$5,949.51
MCY	Mercury General	$39.00	$44.66	$543.36
BCO	Brink's Company	$25.42	$27.33	$282.68
LLL	L3 Technologies	$89.59	$111.31	$912.24
AIZ	Assurant	$37.80	$78.89	$3,944.64
OLN	Olin Corporation	$17.85	$27.44	$2,012.85
TAL	TAL Education	$14.95	$79.30	$16,151.85
CEQP	Crestwood Equity	$13.56	$27.40	$3,958.13
FMC	FMC Corporation	$34.75	$62.12	$2,983.88
MRK	Merck & Company	$40.53	$61.07	$1,910.22

Symbol	Name	Buy Price	Sell Price	Profit
KBR	KBR, Inc.	$20.77	$21.18	$74.21
PEG	PSEG Inc.	$32.60	$50.47	$2,055.55
AXS	Axis Capital	$35.05	$51.72	$1,900.38
COP	ConocoPhillips	$59.28	$60.20	$56.12
WU	Western Union	$13.53	$20.63	$1,901.46
PSO	Pearson	$7.63	$9.79	$1,036.80
SRE	Sempra Energy	$52.66	$116.99	$4,567.08
GM	General Motors	$38.31	$38.87	$54.08
EQR	Equity Residential	$62.00	$71.74	$574.66

RESULTS BY YEAR

2010

Symbol	Name	Buy Price	P/E	Shares	Amount spent
CIM	Chimera	$4.13	2.16	909	$3,751.90
HUN	Huntsman	$12.42	5.47	302	$3,750.84
RNR	RenaissanceRe	$54.48	5.94	69	$3,759.12
AIZ	Assurant	$30.52	6.00	123	$3,753.96
DFS	Discover	$14.73	6.09	255	$3,756.15
MFA	MFA Financial	$7.23	7.02	519	$3,752.37
WH	Wyndham	$3.24	7.20	1,157	$3,748.68
AFG	AFG	$25.38	7.46	148	$3,756.24
NNI	Nelnet	$17.05	7.71	220	$3,751.00
CB	Chubb	$50.02	8.36	75	$3,751.50
BIP	Brookfield	$17.00	8.46	221	$3,757.00
OLN	Olin	$17.85	8.62	210	$3,748.50
RE	Everest	$85.36	8.82	44	$3,755.84
TMK	Torchmark	$46.68	9.10	80	$3,734.40
TRV	Travelers	$48.93	9.11	77	$3,767.61
CF	CF Industries	$97.98	9.86	38	$3,723.24
AEE	Ameren	$27.42	9.97	137	$3,756.54
LMT	Lockheed	$77.49	10.13	48	$3,719.40
PKG	Packaging	$23.75	10.19	158	$3,752.50
UNM	Unum Group	$21.53	10.20	174	$3,746.22
UGI	UGI Corp.	$24.53	10.39	153	$3,753.09
MRK	Merck	$40.53	10.61	93	$3,769.29

Symbol	Name	Buy Price	P/E	Shares	Amount spent
WFC	Wells Fargo	$28.05	10.62	134	$3,758.03
MCY	Mercury	$39.00	10.74	96	$3,744.00
BCO	Brink's	$25.42	10.86	148	$3,762.16
KBR	KBR, Inc.	$20.77	10.99	181	$3,759.37
HI	Hillenbrand	$18.28	11.01	205	$3,747.40
TU	TELUS	$31.85	11.09	118	$3,758.30
ADC	Agree Realty	$23.31	11.15	161	$3,752.91
PEG	PSEG Inc.	$32.60	11.20	115	$3,748.43
SRE	Sempra	$52.66	11.28	71	$3,738.86
ECA	Encana	$34.63	11.28	108	$3,740.04
GD	General D.	$70.40	11.28	53	$3,731.20
MAC	Macerich	$33.45	11.30	112	$3,746.40
TAL	TAL Education	$14.95	11.41	251	$3,752.45
LLL	L3 Tech	$89.59	11.46	42	$3,762.78
EXC	Exelon	$48.73	11.47	77	$3,752.21
RTN	Raytheon	$54.40	11.75	69	$3,753.26
APU	AmeriGas	$41.70	11.62	90	$3,753.00
UNH	UnitedHealth	$35.37	11.67	105	$3,713.33

2010 Shares Sold   (Sell date January 19th, 2011)

Symbol	Name	Sell Price	P/E	Shares	Profit
HUN	Huntsman	$17.58	251.14	302	$1,558.32
CF	CF Ind.	$144.52	42.63	38	$1,768.52
AEE	Ameren	$28.41	42.40	137	$135.63
MAC	Macerich	$47.61	-529	112	$1,585.92

Account Balance Jan 19th, 2011: $180,777.77

2010 Annual return: 20.53%

2011

Symbol	Name	Buy Price	P/E	Shares	Amount spent
CIM	Chimera	$4.13	2.16	909	$3,751.90
RNR	RenaissanceRe	$54.48	5.94	69	$3,759.12
AIZ	Assurant	$30.52	6.00	123	$3,753.96
DFS	Discover	$14.73	6.09	255	$3,756.15
MFA	MFA Financial	$7.23	7.02	519	$3,752.37
WH	Wyndham	$3.24	7.20	1,157	$3,784.68
AFG	AFG	$25.38	7.46	148	$3,756.24
NNI	Nelnet	$17.05	7.71	220	$3,751.00
CB	Chubb	$50.02	8.36	75	$3,751.50
BIP	Brookfield	$17.00	8.46	221	$3,757.00
OLN	Olin	$17.85	8.62	210	$3,748.50
RE	Everest	$85.36	8.82	44	$3,755.84
TMK	Torchmark	$46.68	9.10	120*	$3,734.40
TRV	Travelers	$48.93	9.11	77	$3,767.61
LMT	Lockheed	$77.49	10.13	48	$3,719.40
PKG	Packaging	$23.75	10.19	158	$3,752.50
UNM	Unum Group	$21.53	10.20	174	$3,746.22
UGI	UGI Corp.	$24.53	10.39	153	$3,753.09
MRK	Merck	$40.53	10.61	93	$3,769.29
WFC	Wells Fargo	$28.05	10.62	134	$3,758.03
MCY	Mercury	$39.00	10.74	96	$3,744.00
BCO	Brink's	$25.42	10.86	148	$3,762.16
KBR	KBR, Inc.	$20.77	10.99	181	$3,759.37
HI	Hillenbrand	$18.28	11.01	205	$3,747.40

Symbol	Name	Buy Price	P/E	Shares	Amount spent
TU	TELUS	$31.85	11.09	118	$3,758.30
ADC	Agree Realty	$23.31	11.15	161	$3,752.91
PEG	PSEG Inc.	$32.60	11.20	115	$3,748.43
SRE	Sempra	$52.66	11.28	71	$3,738.86
ECA	Encana	$34.63	11.28	108	$3,740.04
GD	General D.	$70.40	11.28	53	$3,731.20
TAL	TAL Education	$14.95	11.41	251	$3,752.45
LLL	L3 Tech	$89.59	11.46	42	$3,762.78
EXC	Exelon	$48.73	11.47	77	$3,752.21
RTN	Raytheon	$54.40	11.75	69	$3,753.26
APU	AmeriGas	$41.70	11.62	90	$3,753.00
UNH	UnitedHealth	$35.37	11.67	105	$3,713.33
AGO	Assured G.	$19.06	3.45	210	$4,002.62
AVY	Avery D.	$41.79	3.60	96	$4,011.84
BG	Bunge Limited	$71.70	5.59	56	$4,015.20
WY	Weyerhaeuser	$21.51	5.89	186	$4,000.86
AXS	Axis Capital	$35.05	5.92	114	$3,995.70

*TMK 1.5 for 1 stock split

2011 Shares Sold   (Sell date January 19th, 2012)

Symbol	Name	Sell Price	P/E	Shares	Profit
RNR	RenaissanceRe	$72.93	-64.5	69	$1,273.05
ADC	Agree Realty	$25.38	87.52	161	$333.27

Account Balance Jan 19th, 2012:   **$180,170.30**

2011 Annual return: **-0.34%**

2012

Symbol	Name	Buy Price	P/E	Shares	Amount spent
CIM	Chimera	$4.13	2.16	909	$3,751.90
AIZ	Assurant	$30.52	6.00	123	$3,753.96
DFS	Discover	$14.73	6.09	255	$3,756.15
MFA	MFA Financial	$7.23	7.02	519	$3,752.37
WH	Wyndham	$3.24	7.20	1,157	$3,784.68
AFG	AFG	$25.38	7.46	148	$3,756.24
NNI	Nelnet	$17.05	7.71	220	$3,751.00
CB	Chubb	$50.02	8.36	75	$3,751.50
BIP	Brookfield	$17.00	8.46	221	$3,757.00
OLN	Olin	$17.85	8.62	210	$3,748.50
RE	Everest	$85.36	8.82	44	$3,755.84
TMK	Torchmark	$46.68	9.10	120	$3,734.40
TRV	Travelers	$48.93	9.11	77	$3,767.61
LMT	Lockheed	$77.49	10.13	48	$3,719.40
PKG	Packaging	$23.75	10.19	158	$3,752.50
UNM	Unum Group	$21.53	10.20	174	$3,746.22
UGI	UGI Corp.	$24.53	10.39	153	$3,753.09
MRK	Merck	$40.53	10.61	93	$3,769.29
WFC	Wells Fargo	$28.05	10.62	134	$3,758.03
MCY	Mercury	$39.00	10.74	96	$3,744.00
BCO	Brink's	$25.42	10.86	148	$3,762.16
KBR	KBR, Inc.	$20.77	10.99	181	$3,759.37
HI	Hillenbrand	$18.28	11.01	205	$3,747.40
TU	TELUS	$31.85	11.09	118	$3,758.30

Symbol	Name	Buy Price	P/E	Shares	Amount spent
PEG	PSEG Inc.	$32.60	11.20	115	$3,748.43
SRE	Sempra	$52.66	11.28	71	$3,738.86
ECA	Encana	$34.63	11.28	108	$3,740.04
GD	General D.	$70.40	11.28	53	$3,731.20
TAL	TAL Education	$14.95	11.41	251	$3,752.45
LLL	L3 Tech	$89.59	11.46	42	$3,762.78
EXC	Exelon	$48.73	11.47	77	$3,752.21
RTN	Raytheon	$54.40	11.75	69	$3,753.26
APU	AmeriGas	$41.70	11.62	90	$3,753.00
UNH	UnitedHealth	$35.37	11.67	105	$3,713.33
AGO	Assured G.	$19.06	3.45	210	$4,002.62
AVY	Avery D.	$41.79	3.6	96	$4,011.84
BG	Bunge Limited	$71.70	5.59	56	$4,015.20
WY	Weyerhaeuser	$21.51	5.89	186	$4,000.86
AXS	Axis Capital	$35.05	5.92	114	$3,995.70
TRGP	Targa Res.	$41.97	2.87	72	$3,021.84
ITT	ITT Inc.	$22.01	3.21	138	$3,037.38
MFC	Manulife	$11.92	4.70	255	$3,039.60

2012 Shares Sold   (Sell date January 22nd, 2013)

Symbol	Name	Sell Price	P/E	Shares	Profit
BIP	Brookfield	$36.85	70.87	221	$4,386.85
WY	Weyerhaeuser	$30.89	54.19	186	$1,744.68
TRGP	Targa Res.	$59.27	102.19	72	$1,245.60
ITT	ITT Inc.	$25.47	-5.15	138	$477.48
MFC	Manulife	$14.58	51.16	255	$678.30

Account Balance Jan 22nd, 2013: $210,367.95

2012 Annual return: 16.76%

2013

Symbol	Name	Buy Price	P/E	Shares	Amount spent
CIM	Chimera	$4.13	2.16	909	$3,751.90
AIZ	Assurant	$30.52	6.00	123	$3,753.96
DFS	Discover	$14.73	6.09	255	$3,756.15
MFA	MFA Financial	$7.23	7.02	519	$3,752.37
WH	Wyndham	$3.24	7.20	1,157	$3,784.68
AFG	AFG	$25.38	7.46	148	$3,756.24
NNI	Nelnet	$17.05	7.71	220	$3,751.00
CB	Chubb	$50.02	8.36	75	$3,751.50
OLN	Olin	$17.85	8.62	210	$3,748.50
RE	Everest	$85.36	8.82	44	$3,755.84
TMK	Torchmark	$46.68	9.10	120	$3,734.40
TRV	Travelers	$48.93	9.11	77	$3,767.61
LMT	Lockheed	$77.49	10.13	48	$3,719.40
PKG	Packaging	$23.75	10.19	158	$3,752.50
UNM	Unum Group	$21.53	10.20	174	$3,746.22
UGI	UGI Corp.	$24.53	10.39	153	$3,753.09
MRK	Merck	$40.53	10.61	93	$3,769.29
WFC	Wells Fargo	$28.05	10.62	134	$3,758.03
MCY	Mercury	$39.00	10.74	96	$3,744.00
BCO	Brink's	$25.42	10.86	148	$3,762.16
KBR	KBR, Inc.	$20.77	10.99	181	$3,759.37
HI	Hillenbrand	$18.28	11.01	205	$3,747.40
TU	TELUS	$31.85	11.09	236*	$3,758.30
PEG	PSEG Inc.	$32.60	11.20	115	$3,748.43

Symbol	Name	Buy Price	P/E	Shares	Amount spent
SRE	Sempra	$52.66	11.28	71	$3,738.86
ECA	Encana	$34.63	11.28	108	$3,740.04
GD	General D.	$70.40	11.28	53	$3,731.20
TAL	TAL Education	$14.95	11.41	251	$3,752.45
LLL	L3 Tech	$89.59	11.46	42	$3,762.78
EXC	Exelon	$48.73	11.47	77	$3,752.21
RTN	Raytheon	$54.40	11.75	69	$3,753.26
APU	AmeriGas	$41.70	11.62	90	$3,753.00
UNH	UnitedHealth	$35.37	11.67	105	$3,713.33
AGO	Assured G.	$19.06	3.45	210	$4,002.62
AVY	Avery D.	$41.79	3.6	96	$4,011.84
BG	Bunge Limited	$71.70	5.59	56	$4,015.20
AXS	Axis Capital	$35.05	5.92	114	$3,995.70
ALE	Allete	$43.85	1.25	83	$3,639.55
F	Ford	$14.02	3.23	259	$3,631.23
AIZ	Assurant	$37.80	5.37	96	$3,628.80
CLF	Cleveland Cl.	$37.12	5.78	98	$3,637.96
HFC	HollyFrontier	$44.17	6.11	82	$3,621.94
COP	ConocoPhillips	$59.28	6.43	61	$3,616.08
WU	Western Un.	$13.53	6.73	268	$3,626.04

*TU 2 for 1 stock split

2013 Shares Sold   (Sell date January 22nd, 2014)

Symbol	Name	Sell Price	P/E	Shares	Profit
DFS	Discover	$53.39	0*	255	$9,858.30
GD	General D.	$95.94	-135	53	$1,353.62
BG	Bunge	$81.13	-43.8	56	$527.80

*Earnings were zero

Account Balance Jan 22nd, 2014: $262,893.16

2013 Annual return: 24.97%

2014

Symbol	Name	Buy Price	P/E	Shares	Amount spent
CIM	Chimera	$4.13	2.16	909	$3,751.90
AIZ	Assurant	$30.52	6.00	123	$3,753.96
MFA	MFA Financial	$7.23	7.02	519	$3,752.37
WH	Wyndham	$3.24	7.20	1,157	$3,784.68
AFG	AFG	$25.38	7.46	148	$3,756.24
NNI	Nelnet	$17.05	7.71	220	$3,751.00
CB	Chubb	$50.02	8.36	75	$3,751.50
OLN	Olin	$17.85	8.62	210	$3,748.50
RE	Everest	$85.36	8.82	44	$3,755.84
TMK	Torchmark	$46.68	9.10	180*	$3,734.40
TRV	Travelers	$48.93	9.11	77	$3,767.61
LMT	Lockheed	$77.49	10.13	48	$3,719.40
PKG	Packaging	$23.75	10.19	158	$3,752.50
UNM	Unum Group	$21.53	10.20	174	$3,746.22
UGI	UGI Corp.	$24.53	10.39	230*	$3,753.09
MRK	Merck	$40.53	10.61	93	$3,769.29
WFC	Wells Fargo	$28.05	10.62	134	$3,758.03
MCY	Mercury	$39.00	10.74	96	$3,744.00
BCO	Brink's	$25.42	10.86	148	$3,762.16
KBR	KBR, Inc.	$20.77	10.99	181	$3,759.37
HI	Hillenbrand	$18.28	11.01	205	$3,747.40
TU	TELUS	$31.85	11.09	236	$3,758.30
PEG	PSEG Inc.	$32.60	11.20	115	$3,748.43
SRE	Sempra	$52.66	11.28	71	$3,738.86

Symbol	Name	Buy Price	P/E	Shares	Amount spent
ECA	Encana	$34.63	11.28	108	$3,740.04
TAL	TAL Education	$14.95	11.41	251	$3,752.45
LLL	L3 Tech	$89.59	11.46	42	$3,762.78
EXC	Exelon	$48.73	11.47	77	$3,752.21
RTN	Raytheon	$54.40	11.75	69	$3,753.26
APU	AmeriGas	$41.70	11.62	90	$3,753.00
UNH	UnitedHealth	$35.37	11.67	105	$3,713.33
AGO	Assured G.	$19.06	3.45	210	$4,002.62
AVY	Avery D.	$41.79	3.6	96	$4,011.84
AXS	Axis Capital	$35.05	5.92	114	$3,995.70
ALE	Allete	$43.85	1.25	83	$3,639.55
F	Ford	$14.02	3.23	259	$3,631.23
AIZ	Assurant	$37.80	5.37	96	$3,628.80
CLF	Cleveland Cl.	$37.12	5.78	98	$3,637.96
HFC	HollyFrontier	$44.17	6.11	82	$3,621.94
COP	ConocoPhillips	$59.28	6.43	61	$3,616.08
WU	Western Un.	$13.53	6.73	268	$3,626.04
BXMT	Capital Trust	$28.05	0.65	138	$3,870.21
NLY	Annaly Capital	$10.35	3.04	374	$3,870.86
PHM	PulteGroup	$19.33	3.07	200	$3,866.00
MA	Mastercard	$82.02	3.24	47	$3,854.94
CEQP	Crestwood	$13.56	3.47	286	$3,878.27
TWO	Two Harbors	$9.82	5.84	395	$3,873.71

*TMK 1.5 for 1 stock split. UGI 1.5 for 1 stock split.

2014 Shares Sold

No shares were sold for the year.

Account Balance Jan 22nd, 2015: $279,638.79

2014 Annual return: 6.37%

2015

Symbol	Name	Buy Price	P/E	Shares	Amount spent
CIM	Chimera	$4.13	2.16	182*	$3,751.90
AIZ	Assurant	$30.52	6.00	123	$3,753.96
MFA	MFA Financial	$7.23	7.02	519	$3,752.37
WH	Wyndham	$3.24	7.20	1,157	$3,784.68
AFG	AFG	$25.38	7.46	148	$3,756.24
NNI	Nelnet	$17.05	7.71	220	$3,751.00
CB	Chubb	$50.02	8.36	75	$3,751.50
OLN	Olin	$17.85	8.62	210	$3,748.50
RE	Everest	$85.36	8.82	44	$3,755.84
TMK	Torchmark	$46.68	9.10	180	$3,734.40
TRV	Travelers	$48.93	9.11	77	$3,767.61
LMT	Lockheed	$77.49	10.13	48	$3,719.40
PKG	Packaging	$23.75	10.19	158	$3,752.50
UNM	Unum Group	$21.53	10.20	174	$3,746.22
UGI	UGI Corp.	$24.53	10.39	230	$3,753.09
MRK	Merck	$40.53	10.61	93	$3,769.29
WFC	Wells Fargo	$28.05	10.62	134	$3,758.03
MCY	Mercury	$39.00	10.74	96	$3,744.00
BCO	Brink's	$25.42	10.86	148	$3,762.16
KBR	KBR, Inc.	$20.77	10.99	181	$3,759.37
HI	Hillenbrand	$18.28	11.01	205	$3,747.40
TU	TELUS	$31.85	11.09	236	$3,758.30
PEG	PSEG Inc.	$32.60	11.20	115	$3,748.43
SRE	Sempra	$52.66	11.28	71	$3,738.86

Symbol	Name	Buy Price	P/E	Shares	Amount spent
ECA	Encana	$34.63	11.28	108	$3,740.04
TAL	TAL Education	$14.95	11.41	251	$3,752.45
LLL	L3 Tech	$89.59	11.46	42	$3,762.78
EXC	Exelon	$48.73	11.47	77	$3,752.21
RTN	Raytheon	$54.40	11.75	69	$3,753.26
APU	AmeriGas	$41.70	11.62	90	$3,753.00
UNH	UnitedHealth	$35.37	11.67	105	$3,713.33
AGO	Assured G.	$19.06	3.45	210	$4,002.62
AVY	Avery D.	$41.79	3.6	96	$4,011.84
AXS	Axis Capital	$35.05	5.92	114	$3,995.70
ALE	Allete	$43.85	1.25	83	$3,639.55
F	Ford	$14.02	3.23	259	$3,631.23
AIZ	Assurant	$37.80	5.37	96	$3,628.80
CLF	Cleveland Cl.	$37.12	5.78	98	$3,637.96
HFC	HollyFrontier	$44.17	6.11	82	$3,621.94
COP	ConocoPhillips	$59.28	6.43	61	$3,616.08
WU	Western Un.	$13.53	6.73	268	$3,626.04
BXMT	Capital Trust	$28.05	0.65	138	$3,870.21
NLY	Annaly Capital	$10.35	3.04	374	$3,870.86
PHM	PulteGroup	$19.33	3.07	200	$3,866.00
MA	Mastercard	$82.02	3.24	47	$3,854.94
CEQP	Crestwood	$13.56	3.47	286	$3,878.27
TWO	Two Harbors	$9.82	5.84	395	$3,873.71

*CIM 0.2 for 1 stock split

2015 Shares Sold   (Sell date January 25th, 2016)

Symbol	Name	Sell Price	P/E	Shares	Profit
AIZ	Assurant	$78.89	44.02	123	$5,949.51
MCY	Mercury Gen.	$44.66	81.78	96	$543.36
BCO	Brink's	$27.33	-24.2	148	$282.68
LLL	L3 Tech.	$111.31	71.31	42	$912.24
AIZ	Assurant	$78.89	44.02	96	$3,944.64

Account Balance Jan 25th, 2016:   **$249,934.66**

2015 Annual return: **-10.62%**

Note: The annual return figure of -10.62% is misleading since I didn't sell any shares at a loss. I was paid $8,247.61 in dividends and had a profit of $11,632.43 from the shares sold for the year. All it means is that there was a slight downturn in the market.

2016

Symbol	Name	Buy Price	P/E	Shares	Amount spent
CIM	Chimera	$4.13	2.16	182	$3,751.90
MFA	MFA Financial	$7.23	7.02	519	$3,752.37
WH	Wyndham	$3.24	7.20	1,157	$3,784.68
AFG	AFG	$25.38	7.46	148	$3,756.24
NNI	Nelnet	$17.05	7.71	220	$3,751.00
CB	Chubb	$50.02	8.36	75	$3,751.50
OLN	Olin	$17.85	8.62	210	$3,748.50
RE	Everest	$85.36	8.82	44	$3,755.84
TMK	Torchmark	$46.68	9.10	180	$3,734.40
TRV	Travelers	$48.93	9.11	77	$3,767.61
LMT	Lockheed	$77.49	10.13	48	$3,719.40
PKG	Packaging	$23.75	10.19	158	$3,752.50
UNM	Unum Group	$21.53	10.20	174	$3,746.22
UGI	UGI Corp.	$24.53	10.39	230	$3,753.09
MRK	Merck	$40.53	10.61	93	$3,769.29
WFC	Wells Fargo	$28.05	10.62	134	$3,758.03
KBR	KBR, Inc.	$20.77	10.99	181	$3,759.37
HI	Hillenbrand	$18.28	11.01	205	$3,747.40
TU	TELUS	$31.85	11.09	236	$3,758.30
PEG	PSEG Inc.	$32.60	11.20	115	$3,748.43
SRE	Sempra	$52.66	11.28	71	$3,738.86
ECA	Encana	$34.63	11.28	108	$3,740.04
TAL	TAL Education	$14.95	11.41	251	$3,752.45
EXC	Exelon	$48.73	11.47	77	$3,752.21

Symbol	Name	Buy Price	P/E	Shares	Amount spent
RTN	Raytheon	$54.40	11.75	69	$3,753.26
APU	AmeriGas	$41.70	11.62	90	$3,753.00
UNH	UnitedHealth	$35.37	11.67	105	$3,713.33
AGO	Assured G.	$19.06	3.45	210	$4,002.62
AVY	Avery D.	$41.79	3.6	96	$4,011.84
AXS	Axis Capital	$35.05	5.92	114	$3,995.70
ALE	Allete	$43.85	1.25	83	$3,639.55
F	Ford	$14.02	3.23	259	$3,631.23
CLF	Cleveland Cl.	$37.12	5.78	98	$3,637.96
HFC	HollyFrontier	$44.17	6.11	82	$3,621.94
COP	ConocoPhillips	$59.28	6.43	61	$3,616.08
WU	Western Un.	$13.53	6.73	268	$3,626.04
BXMT	Capital Trust	$28.05	0.65	138	$3,870.21
NLY	Annaly Capital	$10.35	3.04	374	$3,870.86
PHM	PulteGroup	$19.33	3.07	200	$3,866.00
MA	Mastercard	$82.02	3.24	47	$3,854.94
CEQP	Crestwood	$13.56	3.47	286	$3,878.27
TWO	Two Harbors	$9.82	5.84	395	$3,873.71
HPQ	HP Inc.	$9.74	3.93	389	$3,786.92
TRN	Trinity	$20.07	4.20	189	$3,793.23
NVO	Novo Nordisk	$55.12	4.31	69	$3,803.28
DAN	Dana Inc.	$11.34	5.32	334	$3,787.56
TGNA	TEGNA	$23.50	5.47	161	$3,783.50
FMC	FMC Corp.	$34.75	6.04	109	$3,787.21
BNS	Nova Scotia B.	$37.57	6.63	101	$3,794.57
MPC	Marathon Pet.	$42.60	6.74	89	$3,791.40

2016 Shares Sold   (Sell date January 25th, 2017)

Symbol	Name	Sell Price	P/E	Shares	Profit
OLN	Olin Corp.	$27.44	-29.5	210	$2,012.85
TAL	TAL Educ.	$79.30	76.25	251	$16,151.85
CEQP	Crestwood	$27.40	-0.64	286	$3,958.13
FMC	FMC Corp	$62.12	-776	109	$2,983.88

Account Balance Jan 25th, 2017:   **$350,356.96**

2016 Annual return: **40.18%**

2017

Symbol	Name	Buy Price	P/E	Shares	Amount spent
CIM	Chimera	$4.13	2.16	182	$3,751.90
MFA	MFA Financial	$7.23	7.02	519	$3,752.37
WH	Wyndham	$3.24	7.20	1,157	$3,784.68
AFG	AFG	$25.38	7.46	148	$3,756.24
NNI	Nelnet	$17.05	7.71	220	$3,751.00
CB	Chubb	$50.02	8.36	75	$3,751.50
RE	Everest	$85.36	8.82	44	$3,755.84
TMK	Torchmark	$46.68	9.10	180	$3,734.40
TRV	Travelers	$48.93	9.11	77	$3,767.61
LMT	Lockheed	$77.49	10.13	48	$3,719.40
PKG	Packaging	$23.75	10.19	158	$3,752.50
UNM	Unum Group	$21.53	10.20	174	$3,746.22
UGI	UGI Corp.	$24.53	10.39	230	$3,753.09
MRK	Merck	$40.53	10.61	93	$3,769.29
WFC	Wells Fargo	$28.05	10.62	134	$3,758.03
KBR	KBR, Inc.	$20.77	10.99	181	$3,759.37
HI	Hillenbrand	$18.28	11.01	205	$3,747.40
TU	TELUS	$31.85	11.09	236	$3,758.30
PEG	PSEG Inc.	$32.60	11.20	115	$3,748.43
SRE	Sempra	$52.66	11.28	71	$3,738.86
ECA	Encana	$34.63	11.28	108	$3,740.04
EXC	Exelon	$48.73	11.47	77	$3,752.21
RTN	Raytheon	$54.40	11.75	69	$3,753.26
APU	AmeriGas	$41.70	11.62	90	$3,753.00

Symbol	Name	Buy Price	P/E	Shares	Amount spent
UNH	UnitedHealth	$35.37	11.67	105	$3,713.33
AGO	Assured G.	$19.06	3.45	210	$4,002.62
AVY	Avery D.	$41.79	3.6	96	$4,011.84
AXS	Axis Capital	$35.05	5.92	114	$3,995.70
ALE	Allete	$43.85	1.25	83	$3,639.55
F	Ford	$14.02	3.23	259	$3,631.23
CLF	Cleveland Cl.	$37.12	5.78	98	$3,637.96
HFC	HollyFrontier	$44.17	6.11	82	$3,621.94
COP	ConocoPhillips	$59.28	6.43	61	$3,616.08
WU	Western Un.	$13.53	6.73	268	$3,626.04
BXMT	Capital Trust	$28.05	0.65	138	$3,870.21
NLY	Annaly Capital	$10.35	3.04	374	$3,870.86
PHM	PulteGroup	$19.33	3.07	200	$3,866.00
MA	Mastercard	$82.02	3.24	47	$3,854.94
TWO	Two Harbors	$9.82	5.84	197*	$3,873.71
HPQ	HP Inc.	$9.74	3.93	389	$3,786.92
TRN	Trinity	$20.07	4.20	189	$3,793.23
NVO	Novo Nordisk	$55.12	4.31	69	$3,803.28
DAN	Dana Inc.	$11.34	5.32	334	$3,787.56
TGNA	TEGNA	$23.50	5.47	161	$3,783.50
BNS	Nova Scotia B.	$37.57	6.63	101	$3,794.57
MPC	Marathon Pet.	$42.60	6.74	89	$3,791.40
LYG	Lloyds Banking	$3.34	1.37	1,098	$3,661.83
GM	General Mot.	$38.31	4.43	96	$3,677.76
RIG	Transocean	$15.33	4.85	239	$3,663.87
AGO	Assured G.	$40.10	5.01	91	$3,649.10

Symbol	Name	Buy Price	P/E	Shares	Amount spent
BAX	Baxter Int.	$46.04	5.16	80	$3,683.20
EQR	Equity Res.	$62.00	5.40	59	$3,658.00
LFC	China Life	$13.74	5.61	266	$3,654.84
PSO	Pearson	$7.63	6.43	480	$3,662.40
CIM	Chimera	$17.70	7.56	207	$3,663.90
CM	CIBC	$85.80	8.02	43	$3,689.40
DAL	Delta Air	$50.27	8.13	73	$3,669.64

*TWO 0.5 for 1 stock split

2017 Shares Sold   (Sell date January 25th, 2018)

Symbol	Name	Sell Price	P/E	Shares	Profit
MRK	Merck	$61.07	58.72	93	$1,910.22
KBR	KBR, Inc.	$21.18	41.53	181	$74.21
PEG	PSEG Inc.	$50.47	49.00	115	$2,055.05
AXS	Axis Capital	$51.72	-17.2	114	$1,900.38
COP	ConocoPhil.	$60.20	-29.9	61	$56.12
WU	Western Un.	$20.63	43.88	268	$1,901.46
PSO	Pearson	$9.79	-3.74	480	$1,036.80

Account Balance Jan 25th, 2018:   **$417,626.69**

2017 Annual return: **19.20%**

2018

Symbol	Name	Buy Price	P/E	Shares	Amount spent
CIM	Chimera	$4.13	2.16	182	$3,751.90
MFA	MFA Financial	$7.23	7.02	519	$3,752.37
WH	Wyndham	$3.24	7.20	1,157	$3,784.68
AFG	AFG	$25.38	7.46	148	$3,756.24
NNI	Nelnet	$17.05	7.71	220	$3,751.00
CB	Chubb	$50.02	8.36	75	$3,751.50
RE	Everest	$85.36	8.82	44	$3,755.84
TMK	Torchmark	$46.68	9.10	180	$3,734.40
TRV	Travelers	$48.93	9.11	77	$3,767.61
LMT	Lockheed	$77.49	10.13	48	$3,719.40
PKG	Packaging	$23.75	10.19	158	$3,752.50
UNM	Unum Group	$21.53	10.20	174	$3,746.22
UGI	UGI Corp.	$24.53	10.39	230	$3,753.09
WFC	Wells Fargo	$28.05	10.62	134	$3,758.03
HI	Hillenbrand	$18.28	11.01	205	$3,747.40
TU	TELUS	$31.85	11.09	236	$3,758.30
SRE	Sempra	$52.66	11.28	71	$3,738.86
ECA	Encana	$34.63	11.28	108	$3,740.04
EXC	Exelon	$48.73	11.47	77	$3,752.21
RTN	Raytheon	$54.40	11.75	69	$3,753.26
APU	AmeriGas	$41.70	11.62	90	$3,753.00
UNH	UnitedHealth	$35.37	11.67	105	$3,713.33
AGO	Assured G.	$19.06	3.45	210	$4,002.62
AVY	Avery D.	$41.79	3.6	96	$4,011.84

Symbol	Name	Buy Price	P/E	Shares	Amount spent
ALE	Allete	$43.85	1.25	83	$3,639.55
F	Ford	$14.02	3.23	259	$3,631.23
CLF	Cleveland Cl.	$37.12	5.78	98	$3,637.96
HFC	HollyFrontier	$44.17	6.11	82	$3,621.94
BXMT	Capital Trust	$28.05	0.65	138	$3,870.21
NLY	Annaly Capital	$10.35	3.04	374	$3,870.86
PHM	PulteGroup	$19.33	3.07	200	$3,866.00
MA	Mastercard	$82.02	3.24	47	$3,854.94
TWO	Two Harbors	$9.82	5.84	197	$3,873.71
HPQ	HP Inc.	$9.74	3.93	389	$3,786.92
TRN	Trinity	$20.07	4.20	189	$3,793.23
NVO	Novo Nordisk	$55.12	4.31	69	$3,803.28
DAN	Dana Inc.	$11.34	5.32	334	$3,787.56
TGNA	TEGNA	$23.50	5.47	161	$3,783.50
BNS	Nova Scotia B.	$37.57	6.63	101	$3,794.57
MPC	Marathon Pet.	$42.60	6.74	89	$3,791.40
LYG	Lloyds Banking	$3.34	1.37	1,098	$3,661.83
GM	General Mot.	$38.31	4.43	96	$3,677.76
RIG	Transocean	$15.33	4.85	239	$3,663.87
AGO	Assured G.	$40.10	5.01	91	$3,649.10
BAX	Baxter Int.	$46.04	5.16	80	$3,683.20
EQR	Equity Res.	$62.00	5.40	59	$3,658.00
LFC	China Life	$13.74	5.61	266	$3,654.84
CIM	Chimera	$17.70	7.56	207	$3,663.90
CM	CIBC	$85.80	8.02	43	$3,689.40
DAL	Delta Air	$50.27	8.13	73	$3,669.64

Symbol	Name	Buy Price	P/E	Shares	Amount spent
PK	Park Hotels	$29.72	2.48	131	$3,892.67
ERF	Enerplus	$11.55	2.50	338	$3,903.90
CVE	Cenovus	$10.67	3.91	366	$3,903.39
NLY	Annaly Capital	$11.03	4.22	354	$3,903.45
NGG	National Grid	$57.17	4.96	68	$3,887.56
DRE	Duke Realty	$25.95	6.24	150	$3,891.75
PTR	PetroChina	$80.99	6.75	48	$3,887.52
EXG	Eaton Vance	$9.75	6.95	400	$3,900.00
TECK	Teck Res.	$29.40	7.05	133	$3,910.20

2018 Shares Sold   **(Sell date Feb 1st, 2019)**

Symbol	Name	Sell Price	P/E	Shares	Profit
SRE	Sempra En.	$116.99	-66.4	71	$4,567.08
GM	General Mot.	$38.87	61.7	96	$54.08
EQR	Equity Res.	$71.74	40.53	59	$574.66

Account Balance Feb 1st, 2019:   **$437,749.94**

2018 Annual return: **4.82%**

Note: In 2018, the S&P 500 lost 6.24%. For most of the year, the S&P 500 went sideways and dropped by 14.90% in the last quarter.

Many analysts were panicking and expected the next major stock market crash, but the reality is that no-one knows where the market will go.

What does this result mean? It simply means that 2018 was a retracement year after a long bull run.

It also means that my stock portfolio is set for a large surge, probably in the next year or two because the P/E ratios for most of the stocks are quite low. If there is a market crash, I will be purchasing as much additional stock as I can afford in stocks that are on sale and holding on to the stocks that I have until they are in profit.

The most important thing to remember is not to panic sell when there is a retracement, or full market collapse. If you don't sell a stock, you won't take a loss.

www.ingramcontent.com/pod-product-compliance
Lightning Source LLC
Chambersburg PA
CBHW060319220326
41598CB00027B/4371